SERIES EDITOR: TONY HO

OSPREY AIRCRAFT OF TH

Pusher Ac
of World War 1

Jon Guttman

OSPREY
PUBLISHING

Front cover
During the afternoon of
22 November 1916, Oblt Stefan
Kirmaier, who had taken command
of *Jasta* 'Boelcke' shortly after
the death of its namesake on
29 October, and who had scored
his 11th victory two days earlier,
was leading four Albatros D IIs
west of Bapaume. 'Five of us were
underway, and we were attacked by
two big squadrons at the same time
over there', Ltn Erwin Böhme
subsequently noted in a letter.
'Each of us had to handle several
opponents. I saw Kirmaier as he
hotly pursued a Vikkers [sic] two-
seater, but had several behind him'.

One of the British flights aloft
that day was from the Royal Flying
Corps' No 24 Sqn. Capt John O
Andrews, in DH 2 5998, was leading
'A' Flight back from a previous scrap
in which his engine had been
damaged when he reported being
attacked at 1310 hrs by a flight of
Albatros scouts that did not actually
open fire on him. Andrews turned
to get on the tail of his lowest
assailant and emptied a drum of
Lewis rounds into it at short range.
2Lt Kelvin Crawford, in DH 2 5925,
also got a few rounds off too before
engine trouble forced him to break
off the engagement and hastily land.

The 'hostile machine', as the RFC
communiqué described it, 'crashed
on our side of the lines near Les
Boeufs'. Crawford, who alighted
nearby, found its remains just
behind the frontline British trenches
near Flers and recovered the two
machine guns, with 500 rounds
each, from the wreck. The pilot,
Kirmaier, had been killed by a bullet
in the back of the head. Coming less
than a month after Hptm Oswald
Boelcke's death, Stefan Kirmaier's
demise was a demoralising loss for
Jasta 'Boelcke'. The next day, the
Staffel got its revenge when Ltn
Manfred von Richthofen shot down
DH 2 5864 after what he called 'the
most difficult battle I have had' for
his 11th victory. His opponent, who
also died from a single bullet in the
back of the head, was Maj Lanoe G
Hawker VC, CO of No 24 Sqn (*Cover
artwork by Mark Postlethwaite*)

First published in Great Britain in 2009 by Osprey Publishing
Midland House, West Way, Botley, Oxford, OX2 0PH
44-02 23rd St, Suite 219, Long Island City, NY 11101, USA
E-mail: info@ospreypublishing.com

© 2009 Osprey Publishing Limited

All rights reserved. Apart from any fair dealing for the purpose of private study,
research, criticism or review, as permitted under the Copyright, Design and
Patents Act 1988, no part of this publication may be reproduced, stored in a
retrieval system, or transmitted in any form or by any means, electronic, electrical, chemical, mechanical, optical, photocopying, recording or otherwise without
prior written permission. All enquiries should be addressed to the publisher.

CIP Data for this publication is available from the British Library

Print ISBN 978 1 84603 417 6
PDF e-book ISBN 978 1 84603 897 6

Edited by Tony Holmes
Page design by Tony Truscott
Cover Artwork by Mark Postlethwaite
Aircraft Profiles by Harry Dempsey
Index by Alan Thatcher
Originated by PDQ Digital Media Solution, Suffolk, UK
Printed and bound in China through Bookbuilders

09 10 11 12 13   11 10 9 8 7 6 5 4 3 2

FOR A CATALOGUE OF ALL BOOKS PUBLISHED BY OSPREY
MILITARY AND AVIATION PLEASE CONTACT:

Osprey Direct, c/o Random House Distribution Center,
400 Hahn Road, Westminster, MD 21157
E-mail: uscustomerservice@ospreypublishing.com

Osprey Direct, The Book Service Ltd, Distribution Centre,
Colchester Road, Frating Green, Colchester, Essex, CO7 7DW
E-mail: customerservice@ospreypublishing.com

www.ospreypublishing.com

Osprey Publishing are supporting the Woodland Trust, the UK's leading
woodland conservation charity, by funding the dedication of trees.

ACKNOWLEDGEMENTS
I would like to thank those colleagues whose invaluable assistance in the
scavenger hunt for photographs and supplementary information made this book
what it is – Frank W Bailey, Jack Eder, Colin Huston, Norman Franks, Phil
Jarrett, William Nungesser, Walter Pieters, Les Rogers, Greg Van Wyngarden
and Aaron Weaver. Thanks also to the late John O Andrews, Gwilym H Lewis
and Thomas G Mapplebeck. This book is dedicated to their memory, and to
their comrades-in-flight.

Pusher Aces of World War 1

CONTENTS

A SIMPLE SOLUTION

The popular image of World War 1 aircraft underwent a swift evolution from floundering motorised kites to relatively fast, sleek biplanes, and even monoplanes, that laid the groundwork for the modern aeroplane as we know it today. Seeming somewhat out of place, however, even amongst the earliest of warplanes are the 'pushers'. These were quaint looking contraptions whose crews rode in nacelles that resembled bathtubs with engines and airscrews (propellers) in the back. Such an arrangement usually required the tail surfaces to be attached to booms or, more often, a lattice of struts and bracing wires whose appearance fairly screamed 'drag', 'slow' and 'ungainly'.

The greater efficiency of tractor aircraft had already been proven before war broke out in August 1914. How then, posterity may be tempted to ask at first glance, can these awkward looking monstrosities have coexisted with more advanced designs over the battlefield for so long? The answer lies in a classic example of form following function.

The first controlled heavier-than-air flight by the Wright Brothers in December 1903 had been achieved using an aeroplane fitted with rear-mounted propellers. This was also the case with the first European flight, made by Brazilian Alberto Santos-Dumont in the autumn of 1906. At a time when the very configuration of the aeroplane was still being defined, the pusher arrangement made sense. It made even more sense when thoughts turned to the aeroplane's first military application as a means of scouting and intelligence gathering. Where better to put an observer than up front, where he could have an uninterrupted panoramic view forward and in all directions but aft?

So it was that at the very start of the war French Voisin and Farman pushers shared the skies over the Western Front with tractor reconnaissance aeroplanes such as the British BE 2 and the German Albatros B II. Then in late August 1914 some airmen decided to stop sharing and start shooting.

The quest for control of the skies was initially pursued in one of three ways – mounting a machine gun to fire above or around the propeller; devising a means of synchronising the weapon with the engine so it only fired when the prop was not in the way; and literally avoiding the problem by putting the engine behind the machine gun. The last, seemingly simplest, method lent the pusher aeroplane a renewed martial validity. Indeed, it led to a series of Allied pusher fighters that were able to hold their own against their German counterparts – including the Fokker Eindeckers, with their synchronised machine guns – until 1917, when the gap in performance between them and their tractor-engined counterparts became indisputably hopeless.

Until then, pushers made history. The first destruction of an aeroplane in air-to-air combat using firearms was achieved from the nacelle of a French Voisin 3LA on 5 October 1914. Belgium's first ace scored his first five victories in two-seat pushers. Britain's first production fighter, the Vickers FB 5 Gunbus, earned one of its pilots a Victoria Cross (VC), and

A Voisin 3LA preserved at the *Musée de l'Air et l'Espace* at Le Bourget, in France, demonstrates the pusher's approach to mounting a forward-firing machine gun, while the Nieuport 11 behind it, with its above-the-wing mounting, represents another (*Jon Guttman*)

made such an impression in 1915 that when in doubt the Germans referred to nearly every British pusher they encountered as a 'Vickers'.

In mid-1916 Maj Lanoe G Hawker's No 24 Sqn, with its Airco DH 2s, became the first single-seat fighter unit in the Royal Flying Corps (RFC). DH 2s were involved, directly or indirectly, in the deaths of pioneer German aces Otto Parschau and Oswald Boelcke, and of *Staffelführer* Stefan Kirmaier – and, on the debit side, in the rise of his most famous protegé, the future 'Red Baron' Manfred von Richthofen. One DH 2 pilot, Lionel W B Rees of No 32 Sqn, also earned the VC.

The most successful pushers of them all, however, were large two-seaters built by the Royal Aircraft Factory – the FE 2b and FE 2d. Even as late as mid-1917, their crews were demonstrating how deceptive their ungainly appearance was, with exploits that included the valour that earned Flt Sgt Thomas Mottershead a posthumous VC. Moreover, 'Fees' were credited with killing German aces Hans Berr, Max Immelmann, Gustav Leffers, Karl-Emil Schäfer, Kurt Schneider, Alfred Ulmer and Ernst Wiessner, and with wounding the 'Red Baron' himself.

FIRST BLOOD

Powered flight was not yet seven years old when, on 23 July 1910, August Euler was issued with German Patent DRP 248.601 for a fixed, forward-firing machine gun mounting for an aeroplane. Later that same year, Gabriel Voisin raised a few eyebrows and some skeptical amusement when he displayed a sketchy mount for a 37 mm naval cannon on one of his pusher biplanes. In Britain, Capt Bertram Dickson wrote a memorandum to the standing sub-committee of the Committee of Imperial Defence, advising that the use of aircraft in time of war to gather intelligence 'would lead to the inevitable result of a war in the air, for supremacy of the air, by armed aeroplanes against each other'.

Serious efforts to make Dickson's concept a reality began in 1912. On 7 and 8 June, US Army Capt Charles De Forest Chandler demonstration-fired a Lewis machine gun that had been rigged to a Wright Model B, piloted by Lt Thomas DeWitt Milling, at ground targets. In Britain on 24 July, Geoffrey de Havilland flew a 'Farman Experimental' FE 2 that he had designed for the Royal Aircraft Factory, the aeroplane being powered by a rotary engine and boasting a mounting for a machine gun in the front observer's cockpit.

In that same year, Vickers' newly created aviation branch received an order from the Admiralty after the recent creation of the Naval Wing of the RFC. The Royal Navy wanted a 'fighting biplane' that was armed with a machine gun for offensive, rather than defensive, purposes. After some consideration, the firm opted for a two-seat pusher with a 7.7 mm Maxim gun in a ball-and-socket mounting (which offered 60 degrees of elevation and traverse) in the nose of a two-seat nacelle. Dubbed the 'EFB Destroyer', Vickers' 'Experimental Fighter Biplane' featured unequal-span, forward staggered wings that employed wing warping for lateral control and paired tail surfaces. Power was provided by a 60-80 hp Wolseley V8 engine and the airframe made extensive use of steel tube and aluminium skinning.

The EFB was first exhibited at the Aero Show in Olympia, London, in February 1913, but when it underwent gun testing at Joyce Green, the Destroyer briefly left the ground and then promptly nosed over. Undeterred, Vickers produced an EFB 2 that had increased lower wingspan, no stagger, a 100 hp Gnome monosoupape rotary engine and a new nacelle with celluloid side windows, but the same ball-and-socket Maxim gun mount. This machine also eventually crashed, at Bognor, in October 1913, but not before it had been flown frequently at Brooklands by Capt Herbert F Wood (the company's technical adviser) and Vickers' chief pilot Harold Barnwell.

Next came the EFB 3, also fitted with a 100 hp Gnome monosoupape rotary engine. After a decent showing at the Olympia Aero Show in March 1914, Vickers received a six-aeroplane order from the Admiralty – this contract was taken over by the War Officer upon the start of the conflict in Europe. Vickers continued development with the EFB 4, which featured a more streamlined nacelle and only two tail booms. The single prototype flew in July 1914.

The first of Vickers' efforts to dispense with its 'experimental' status was the FB 5, which again used a 100 hp Gnome monosoupape and mounted a 0.303-in Lewis machine gun atop the front of the observer's pit. Dubbed the Gunbus, this Vickers offering attracted production contracts for both the Royal Naval Air Service (RNAS) and the RFC on 14 August 1914, although examples would not reach the front in force for more than 11 months.

By then the RFC had claimed more aerial combat 'firsts' with its pushers. On 22 August 1914, Lts Louis Aubon Strange and L Penn-Gaskell of No 5 Sqn, flying Farman F 20 No 341, claimed to have fired at a German 'Taube' or 'Aviatik'. Three days later, Lt Hubert D Harvey-Kelly of No 2 Sqn, flying a BE 2a, encountered a Rumpler Taube, which he and his observer, Lt W H C Mansfield, assailed with small arms until its unnerved crew landed near Le Cateau and ran into a nearby wood!

Sgt Joseph Frantz and *Soldat* Louis Quénault were the pilot-observer team who used a Voisin 3LA to achieve the first official air-to-air shoot-down in aviation history on 5 October 1914. Their opponent, Albatros B II B114/14, crashed near Reims, killing Sgt Wilhelm Schilling and Oblt Fritz von Zangen of *Flieger Abteilung* 18 (*Musée de l'Air*)

Adj Charles Nungesser in his Voisin 3LAS, with a rack of bombs installed on one side of the nacelle (*W L Nungesser from the Nungesser family collection via Musée de l'Air et de l'Espace*)

Harvey-Kelly and Mansfield landed nearby, and after a failed attempt at pursuit they returned to the Taube, took some trophies from it, set it on fire and took off for home.

Twenty-four hours later, on the eastern front, *Stabs-Kapitan* Piotr Nikolaevich Nesterov of the Imperial Russian Air Service – who had flown a Nieuport IV through history's first loop on 9 September 1913, only to be rewarded with ten days in jail for 'undue risk with a machine, the property of his government' – destroyed an enemy aeroplane by more extreme means. On 25 August an Austro-Hungarian Albatros had bombed the aerodrome at which Nesterov's unit (the 11th Detachment of the 3rd Aviation Company) was based near the town of Zholkov. When it returned on the 26th, he took off in Morane-Saulnier Type G two-seat monoplane No 281 and, after making two fruitless attacks using a pistol, dived at the Albatros and rammed it. The Austrian crew of Fw Franz Malina and Oblt Friedrich *Freiherr* Rosenthal was killed, but so was Nesterov.

The first actual shooting down of an aeroplane by another occurred on 5 October 1914 when a Voisin 3LA two-seat pusher of French *escadrille* V24, flown by Sgt Joseph Frantz and *Sapeur* Louis Quénault, attacked an Aviatik two-seater over Jonchery-sur-Vesle, near Reims. Armed with an 8 mm Hotchkiss M1909 machine gun, Quénault expended two 48-round magazines but failed to get a decisive hit prior to exhausting his supply of ammunition. By then the German crew was firing back at the Frenchmen with rifles, so Quénault produced one of his own and managed to hit the enemy pilot. The Aviatik subsequently crashed, killing Sgt Wilhelm Schlichting and Obltn Fritz von Zangen of *Feldflieger Abteilung* (*FFA*) 18.

Nungesser (left) and his observer pose behind a German cross, cut from the wing of their victim, that has been draped over the nacelle bow of what is presumably the Voisin in which they shot their Albatros down on the night of 31 July 1915. Nungesser's feat, achieved in an unauthorised flight, earned him the *Croix de Guerre* and eight days' confinement to quarters (*W L Nungesser from the Nungesser family collection via Musée de l'Air et de l'Espace*)

After that the struggle for dominance over the Western Front escalated in deadly earnest. The most effective weapon for accomplishing the task was the machine gun, but the most efficient way of using it remained to be ascertained. Under the circumstances, there were initially two schools of thought regarding fighting aircraft – large flying fortresses with anything from one to three gunner's positions, and single-seat scouts in which the pilot aimed his gun by turning the aeroplane itself nose-first toward the target. Ultimately, the latter came to be recognised as the best way to achieve success in aerial combat, but the problem of clearing the propeller arc remained to be solved.

In 1915, France developed a stable of single-seat tractor '*avions de chasse*', initially using steel wedges on the propellers to deflect the machine gun bullets, or mounting the gun above the wing to clear the airscrew, before adopting synchronised interrupter gear in 1916. One of its leading fighter pilots, however, was to score his first success in the same lumbering Voisin as Frantz and Quénault had flown back in 1914.

Charles Eugène Jules Marie Nungesser was an exuberant man of the world who had raced cars, boxed and learned to fly while in Argentina before the war. Enlisting in the *2e Régiment de Hussards* after war broke out, he ambushed and killed the four occupants of a Mors automobile on 3 September and drove it back to French lines, earning himself the *Médaille Militaire* and the car. Transferring into aviation in November, Nungesser earned his military pilot's brevet at Avord on 15 March 1915, and on 8 April he joined VB106, with whom he flew 53 bombing missions. Nungesser decorated the front nacelle of at least one of his Voisins with a black skull and crossbones, which, later rendered in white with two candles and a coffin within a black heart, became his macabre trademark.

Nungesser chats with his mechanic – and frequent observer-gunner – Roger Pochon in front of their Voisin LAS, now sporting the first version of the death's head that would become the future ace's trademark in the years to come. Nungesser may have applied this after scoring his first of an eventual 43 confirmed victories (*W L Nungesser from the Nungesser family collection via Musée de l'Air et de l'Espace*)

Although they had a superb forward field of fire, pushers were vulnerable to attack from the rear – a problem that became very acute when the Fokker E I, with its synchronised forward firing machine gun, burst upon the scene in mid-1915. The crew of this Farman F 40 of *escadrille* MF44, personally marked with the intriguing Latin legend *QUO VADIS* IV ('Where are you going?'), tried to address the problem by installing an extra Lewis machine gun on a pole to fire back over the upper wing – a standard feature on Britain's Royal Aircraft Factory FE 2b (*Service Historique de l'Armée de l'Air B77/89*)

In the early morning hours of 31 July, Adj Nungesser and his mechanic Roger Pochon went up in a Voisin 3LAS armed with a Hotchkiss machine gun. It was an unauthorised flight, since Nungesser was then on standby duty, but as fortune would have it, five Albatros two-seaters staged a raid on Nancy that night and the Voisin crew caught one, attacked it and sent the aircraft crashing to the ground. For deserting his post, Nungesser was confined to quarters for eight days. For downing the enemy aeroplane he was awarded the *Croix de Guerre*. Soon thereafter, to make more productive use of the hell-raising attitude he had exhibited from the onset, Nungesser's commanding officer sent him for training in single-seat Nieuports.

Flying thereafter in N65, with occasional sojourns with N124 and on his own lone roving commission, Charles Nungesser went on to become France's third-ranking ace with 43 victories. On 8 May 1927 he and navigator François Coli departed Paris in a Levasseur PL 8 biplane christened *L'Oiseau Blanc* in an attempt to fly across the Atlantic Ocean nonstop, only to vanish into legend.

One of several French attempts to develop a pusher fighter was the Breguet BLC. Powered by a 220 hp Renault 12Gd engine and armed with a 37 mm cannon or Lewis machine gun, BLCs were issued in odd lots to various *escadrilles* – in this case V21 at Port-sur-Saône in January 1916 – but were probably withdrawn long before they were officially declared obsolete in November 1916 (*SHAA B86/621*)

BELGIUM'S FIRST ACE

O n 1 April 1915, French prewar aviator Sous-Lt Roland Garros of *escadrille* MS26 shot down an Albatros over Westkappelle, killing Gfr August Spacholz and Ltn Werner Grosskopf of *FFA* 40. He was was flying a Morane Saulnier L parasol monoplane fitted with a forward-firing Hotchkiss machine gun and steel wedges installed behind the propeller blades to deflect whatever rounds struck them. He scored two more victories on 15 and 18 April, but on the latter date the damage he inflicted on his own aeroplane forced him to land behind enemy line at Inglemunster, in Belgium.

Impressed by Garros' brief rampage, the Germans sought to copy his deflector system, but Dutch designer Anthony Fokker came up with a better idea by adapting cam-activated interrupter gear developed by Swiss engineer Franz Schneider to the Eindecker, or monoplanes, that he was producing for the Germans. By the end of July the Fokker E I was establishing the fundamentals for future fighters – a single-seat tractor airframe using mechanical or, in a later case, hydraulic synchronisation to interrupt the machine gun's fire whenever a propeller blade was in front of it.

In the same month that Garros began blazing the trail toward that formula, an unlikely Farman pusher crew was scoring the first aerial victory for Belgium's little 'air corps-in-exile'. The pilot concerned was certainly as aggressive as Garros, but hardly possessed of the 'hunter's eye' deemed essential for a successful fighter pilot. In fact, Fernand Jacquet suffered from myopia, forcing him to rely on glasses to see the ground and on the marksmanship of his observers to survive in the air! Yet in spite of his nearsightedness, Jacquet was destined to become Belgium's first ace, and to ultimately lead its first *Groupe de Chasse*.

Born in Petite Chapelle, in Namur province, to a wealthy landowning family on 2 November 1888, Fernand Maximillian Léon Jacquet entered the Military Academy in October 1907. Upon earning his commission as an infantry officer, he joined the *4e Régiment de Ligne* at Bruges on 25 June 1910. Enthused by aviation, he took up training and duly obtained pilot's brevet No 68 on 25 February 1913, after which Jacquet joined the *2e Escadrille*.

The outbreak of war, and subsequent violation of Belgian neutrality by the Germans, found Lt Jacquet in the *Escadrille* Demanet (I) at Liège. His first reconnaissance sortie on 4 August 1914 was prematurely terminated by a forced landing at Maibelle 30 minutes later. On the 6th Jacquet had his first encounter with a German counterpart – a Taube – over Huy. Five days later enemy ground fire forced him to land at Oostkerke. During the course of these flights Jacquet recognised and reported the danger that the advancing German forces posed to the fortresses in and around Namur.

Lts Fernand Jacquet and Louis Robin pose before a Farman F 40 bearing an elaborate death's head marking (*Walter Pieters*)

When he was not flying, Jacquet often roamed the front in a car armed with a Lewis gun manned by Joseph-Philippe-François de Riquet, Prince de Caraman-Chimay. Between those activities, his previous forced landing and the occupation of his country by the German invaders, Jacquet developed a strong desire to seek vengeance in the air. In addition to his reconnaissance flights, Jacquet sought permission to go on '*missions speciales*', which in essence was to say that he was zealously looking for trouble. On 24 November 1914 Jacquet, now in the *1e Escadrille*, dropped a bomb on Groote Hemme, and on Christmas Eve he delivered more such 'holiday fireworks' to the Germans at Beerst and Eessen.

While the average Farman pilot was content to bring the intelligence or photographs safely home, Jacquet regularly penetrated German territory in the hope of disrupting enemy operations behind the frontline. On 26 February 1915, for example, he took on 10 Aviatiks over La Panne. On 29 March he chased an Aviatik over the Yser River and on the 31st he and a former member of the *5ème Régiment des Lanciers*, Lt Louis Marie Omer August Robin, engaged another Aviatik.

Jacquet finally drew blood on 17 April 1915 while flying a Farman HF 20 powered by an 80 hp Renault engine and armed with a Lewis gun mounted on the right side of the nacelle. His observer, Lt Henri de

The 8 July 1916 issue of *The War Illustrated* included a photo essay of the interception and destruction of a German intruder by Lts Fernand Jacquet and Louis Robin, flying a Maurice Farman MF 11bis, on 20 May (*Walter Pieters*)

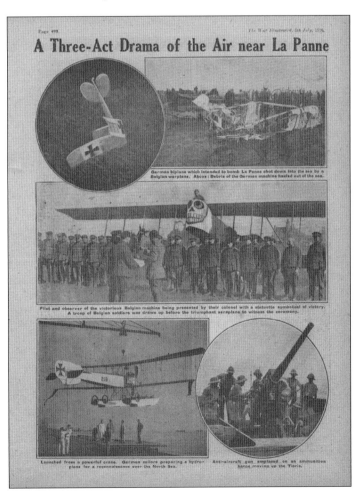

Vindevoghel, was an artillery officer who had requested a transfer to the budding flying corps on 15 December 1914. He also served as the *1e Escadrille's* armourer.

Spotting an Albatros two-seater at 6000 ft – a little below him, and flying a parallel course – Jacquet descended on the enemy, but at a range of 100 yards the German observer fired first, with a carbine. Jacquet continued to close, and at 30 yards Vindevoghel shot off seven rounds, one of which apparently struck the pilot because the Albatros dived into the ground near Beerst. This may have been another aeroplane from *FFA* 40, which reported the loss of Offstv Wilhelm Wohlmacher, killed near Steenstraate, south of Beerst, while his observer, Hptm Bogislav von Hayden, was captured. With the confirmation of his, and Belgium's, first aerial victory, Jacquet redeclared open season on his Teutonic counterparts on 29 April when he chased an enemy aeroplane over Cortemarck.

Somewhere along the way airmen of the *1e Escadrille* began decorating the nacelles of their Farmans with personal markings, and Jacquet, embracing his self-styled avocation of aerial corsair, adorned all of his aeroplanes with a large death's head. If German crews regarded the striking image of a grinning skull on the bow of an oncoming Farman more comic than intimidating, at least four would regret doing so.

Jacquet, with Lt Léon Colignon up front, sent an aeroplane down out of control on 20 June and forced an Aviatik to land near Gits on 28 July, but he had to wait more than a year for his next confirmed victory.

During a morning patrol on 20 May 1916, he and Lt Robin ran into a German floatplane at an altitude of almost 9000 ft and chased it off. Later that same day during an evening sortie, they were surrounded by ten more enemy floatplanes. As Jacquet careened into one flight of five, Robin's gunfire scored hits on the second aeroplane in the formation and sent the third down to crash near Nieuport.

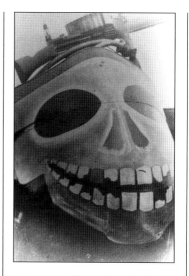

A close-up of the striking death's head marking that adorned the Farman F 40 assigned to Lts Jacquet and Robin in 1916 (*Walter Pieters*)

Robin (left) and Jacquet (centre) suit up for a mission in their Farman F 40 in June 1916. On the 23rd of that month, the two Belgians attacked four LVG two-seaters and three escorting Fokkers. They were subsequently credited with downing one of the Eindeckers for Jacquet's third victory (*Walter Pieters*)

More unconfirmed successes followed on 26 and 27 May and 22 June. Then, on 23 June, Jacquet and Robin attacked a formation of three Fokkers and four LVG two-seaters. Their Farman F 40 was badly shot-up, but Robin managed to drive a Fokker down out of control, which frontline observers later reported as destroyed.

After two further 'probable' claims, on 28 July Jacquet and Robin chased an LVG away from Langemarck, then attacked a German kite balloon with flechettes and finished the afternoon by strafing Ghistelles aerodrome. Taking off on an offensive patrol at 1315 hrs on the 30th, they attacked two LVGs over the Houthulst Forest, driving one away and forcing the other to land near Gits.

Returning to base at 1500 hrs to refuel, Jacquet and Robin were up again 30 minutes later to find an Aviatik engaging a Farman F 40 crewed by Sgt Barthes and *Méchanicen* Baudoin of French *escadrille* MF36. The Belgians drove the German away at 1615 hrs, and 15 minutes later they and their French partners encountered two more LVGs, which they promptly attacked. One of the latter withdrew but the other LVG crashed between Houthulst and Zarren, its demised being credited to both Allied crews. This aircraft may have been from *Kampfstaffel* (or *Kasta*) 2 of *Kagohl* (*Kampfgeschwader Oberste Heeres Leitung*) 1, which reported that pilot Oblt Franz Josef Walz had suffered severe wounds.

—'ACEDOM' IN A BELGIAN-BUILT PUSHER—

Jacquet finally got his chance to become Belgium's first ace while flying in a more or less indigenous aeroplane. After purchasing ten French Farman F 40s in 1916, the Belgians decided to produce their own pusher, redesigned by their military workshop under the direction of Lt Georges Nélis. Designated the GN 1, its redesigned nacelle accommodated a 130 hp Gnome-Rhône rotary engine instead of the F 40's 130 hp water-cooled Renault 8C, equal-span wings with raked tips and a simpler undercarriage similar to that of British pusher types. The GN 2 had a more streamlined nacelle than its predecessor. Some six prototype GNs were built by the French-based Belgian Bollekens firm.

Jacquet and Robin were probably flying the GN 1 when they attacked and indecisively engaged an enemy aeroplane over Bixschoote on 8 September 1916, shortly after which they were struck by anti-aircraft fire

A redesign of the French Farman pusher by Belgian Lt Georges Nélis, the GN 2 featured a reconfigured nacelle, raked wingtips and a simplified, British-inspired undercarriage (*Walter Pieters*)

15

A rear view of the GN 2, showing the 130 hp Gnome-Rhône rotary engine that replaced the Farman F 40's water-cooled 130 hp Renault 8C (*Walter Pieters*)

and brought down. The GN was demolished, but its crewmen emerged without serious injury. In fact, they were patrolling in a replacement aircraft (apparently the GN 2), decorated with Jacquet's death's head, on 24 and 25 September.

In December 1916 Capt Jacquet was named to replace Capt Arsène Demanet as commander of the *1e Escadrille de Chasse*, although Belgian 'ace of aces' Willy Coppens, Baron d'Houthulst, later stated that it was under less-than-auspicious circumstances. According to him, Lt Robin

Lts Jacquet and Robin pose before the GN 2, on which a sketch of Jacquet's trademark skull can just be seen drawn out prior to painting. On 1 February 1917 Jacquet became Belgium's first ace in this machine when he and Robin shot down a brown Rumpler two-seater near Lomardszijde. Their victim may have been from *Fl Abt (A)* 213, which reported observer Lt Fritz Patheiger killed near Polygon Forest that day (*Walter Pieters*)

had addressed Demanet with impertinence and the captain had slapped him across the face, hoping that would chasten him in lieu of a court martial – the latter would have deprived the squadron of one of its finest observer-gunners. Failing to see things that way, the 23-year-old Robin (who, in Coppens' opinion, 'should have been thrashed on his backside') lodged a complaint higher up the army chain of command, resulting in Demanet – a good, experienced pilot and squadron leader – being transferred back to his old artillery unit. The farce ended on a tragic note when Demanet was killed in action on 10 November 1918 – just one day before hostilities ceased.

Jacquet and Robin were still flying the GN 2 on 1 February 1917 when, during their second offensive patrol of the day, they engaged a brown Rumpler two-seater at 12,500 ft and sent it crashing at Lombardsijde at 1515 hrs. Their victim may have been from *FFA (A)* 213, which reported observer Ltn Fritz Patheiger killed near Polygon Wood.

Such was Jacquet's reputation that on 18 March 1917 he became the first pilot entrusted with flying King Albert I over the frontlines, escorted by five Nieuports. When three *escadrilles* were organised into a Belgian *Groupe de Chasse* in March 1918, Jacquet was named its commander at the king's personal insistence.

By then the obsolete pushers were thoroughly unsuitable for the fighting role, but Jacquet's efforts to obtain a Bristol F 2B Fighter were rejected, since it had not been adopted as a standard type by the Belgians. The best he could manage were Sopwith 1A2 and later SPAD XI two-seat reconnaissance aeroplanes. Still, with Lt Marcel de Crombrugghe de Looringhe as his observer, Jacquet managed to drive a Fokker Dr I down out of control on 3 June 1918, forced a Rumpler down on 4 October and repeated the performance over another two-seater on 6 November. The latter two were credited as Jacquet's sixth and seventh victories.

Meanwhile, Lt Robin had qualifed as a pilot in late 1917 and joined the *10ème Escadrille*. Flying 18 sorties and engaging in 11 combats in SPAD XIIIs, his only success was a two-seater forced to land at Zelzate, in the Netherlands, on 3 November 1918, and even that remained unconfirmed. This left his final tally at four, all scored as Jacquet's observer.

Promoted to *capitaine-commandant* in December 1917, Jacquet was awarded the *Croix de Guerre* with six citations, eight *chevrons de front*, *Croix Civil 3e Classe*, *Medaillle de Victoire* and the *Medaille de Commemoration 1914-1918*. He was also made a *Chévalier de l'Ordre de Léopold I*, *Officier de l'Ordre de la Couronne* and later of that same order, with *Palme*. Additionally, the French made him a *Chevalier de la Légion d'Honneur*, and he received their *Croix de Guerre*, the Russian St Anna Order and the only British Distinguished Flying Cross awarded to a Belgian.

In 1920 Jacquet left the army to found a flying school at Gosselies, near Charleroi, the following year, assisted by his former observer Robin. When the Germans invaded Belgium again in World War 2, Jacquet became actively engaged in the resistance until he was arrested in 1942 and imprisoned in Huy Fortress. Robin, a major commanding an armoured car unit in May 1940, was also held prisoner until June 1945. Fernand Jacquet died in Beaumont on 12 October 1947. Robin, who retired from the Belgian army with the rank of colonel in June 1946, died at Etterbeek on 9 August 1976.

Capt Jacquet, commanding the 1st *Groupe de Chasse*, poses with the SPAD XI in which he scored his sixth and seventh victories in 1918 (*Jon Guttman*)

BRITAIN'S FIRST FIGHTERS

W hile the French and Germans strove to develop effective single-seat tractor fighters, the RFC's fighter force was evolving along a pusher path. On 5 February 1915, the first Vickers FB 5 (No 1621) arrived in France. It was flown by 2Lt M R Chidson, who, flying FB 4 No 664 over the Thames Esturary on 24 December 1914, had claimed a Friedrichshafen FF 29 floatplane, although it had in fact got away. FB 5 1621 was initially assigned to No 2 Sqn, but on the 10th it was passed on to No 16 Sqn. Just 18 days later, Chidson and his observer, 2Lt D C W Sanders, were forced to land behind German lines, where they were taken prisoner. Britain's first fighter had duly fallen into enemy hands virtually intact.

During the spring and early summer of 1915, more FB 5s reached the front and were allocated to various units to defend the RFC's reconnaissance aeroplanes and harass those flown by the enemy. On 25 July 1915, No 11 Sqn became the first unit in France to be entirely equipped with FB 5s when it arrived at Vert Galand aerodrome from Netheravon.

Britain's first specialised fighter squadron had come none too soon, since Fokker E Is were just starting their own rampage among Allied reconnaissance units. Nor did No 11 Sqn's men waste much time in rising to the challenge. On 28 July Capt L W B Rees and Flt Sgt J M Hargreaves, in FB 5 1649, drove down one of the vaunted Eindeckers.

Photographed at Farnborough with Frank W Gooden in the cockpit on 24 December 1914, first production Vickers FB 5 Gunbus 1616 wears an early camouflage paint scheme and a small Union Flag on the rudder. Given the presentation legend *DOMINICA* on 13 January 1915, it was allocated to No 5 Sqn RFC and scored several aerial victories before being struck off charge on 10 September (*Phil Jarrett*)

An FB 5 with its pilot, believed to be from No 5 Sqn. This machine features an enlarged rudder and roundels on the underside of the wing inboard of the ailerons (*Greg VanWyngarden*)

An officer in the Royal Garrison Artillery since 1903 who had served in the West African Frontier Force in 1913-14, before joining the RFC on 10 August 1914, Welsh-born Lionel Wilmot Brabazon Rees asserted his aggressive nature over the next few months, ably abetted by Hargreaves. On 31 August they destroyed an LVG C II near Achiet le Grand and then drove down an Ago C I on 21 September, followed by an Albatros the next day. On 30 September they forced an Albatros down in British lines at Gommecourt, the crew, Ltn d R Fritz Kölpin and Oblt Ernst Leonhardi of *FFA* 23, dying of their wounds. Rees was awarded the Military Cross (MC) and Hargreaves the Distinguished Conduct Medal (DCM) for their exploits.

On 31 October Rees and another observer, Flt Sgt Raymond, downed an LVG. With six victories to his credit at that point, Rees was the only pilot to 'make ace' in the Vickers Gunbus, but another FB 5 pilot was to earn Britain's highest honour.

On 6 September Lt Gilbert Stuart Martin Insall and 2Lt G Manley attacked two LVGs, forcing one to dive away and the other to flee eastward. Exactly two weeks later No 11 Sqn moved from Vert Galand to Villers Bretonneux aerodrome. On 7 November, Insall was flying from here in FB 5 5074, with 1st Class Air Mechanic (1AM) T H Donald as his observer, when they attacked an Aviatik near Achiet le Grand. After a merry chase they forced it to land

At the end of an already eventful sortie on 7 November 1915, Lt Gilbert S M Insall's FB 5 5074 was hit in the petrol tank. Insall force landed just 500 yards inside Allied lines, where he and his observer, 1AM T H Donald, remained with their aeroplane under enemy shellfire and then spent the night repairing it, before flying it back to their aerodrome the next morning. Insall was subsequently awarded the VC and Donald the DCM. The two were brought down wounded and taken prisoner on 14 December, but Insall eventually escaped. In 1918 he commanded 'A' Flight of No 51 (Home Defence) Sqn at Bekesbourne (*Norman Franks*)

19

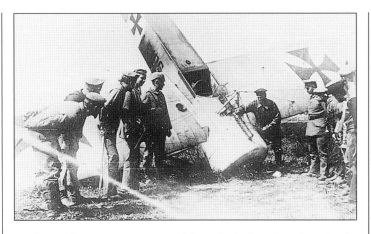

German personnel examine a Fokker E I after a minor accident. This was often the outcome of British claims of enemy aircraft 'down out of control', or 'forced to land' on the enemy side of the lines. Although awarded as victories to the Allied pilots concerned, often the German pilot and his aircraft were only briefly sidelined from the war effort (*Jon Guttman*)

southeast of Arras. Ignoring ground fire – including shots from by the enemy aircrew, at whom Donald returned fire, sending them fleeing from their aeroplane – Insall descended to drop a small incendiary bomb which set the Aviatik afire. On the way home they strafed the German trenches, but return fire holed their petrol tank.

Insall landed in a wood 500 yards inside Allied lines, where he and Donald stood by their aeroplane despite being subjected to 150 well-directed artillery shells. That night, working by torches and other lights, the duo somehow managed to repair their machine and at dawn the next day they took off and returned to their aerodrome.

On 23 December Insall was awarded the VC for his actions, while Donald received the DCM. Neither man was there to receive them, however, having been brought down wounded and taken prisoner nine days earlier either by ground fire or by an enemy two-seater that they had engaged, crewed by ace-to-be Hptm Martin Zander and Ltn Gerche of *FFA* 9b.

After two failed attempts, Insall and two companions escaped from Strohen prison camp on 28 August 1917 and reached the Dutch border nine nights later. Awarded the MC, in mid-1918 Capt Insall returned to service commanding 'A' Flight of No 51 (Home Defence) Sqn at Bekesbourne.

Remaining in Royal Air Force service until 30 July 1945, Gilbert Insall died at Bawtry on 17 February 1972. His gallant Scottish observer, Donald, had died on 22 November 1945.

On 19 November 1915 the second all-FB 5 unit, No 18 Sqn, reached France. By then the Gunbus had made enough of an impression for the Germans to identify any pusher fighter they encountered as a 'Vickers', but with a maximum speed of 70 mph at 5000 ft and a service ceiling of no more than 9000 ft, it was soon outclassed by its single-seat opposition. On 16 March 1916 the RFC's commander, Maj Gen Hugh Trenchard, wrote to the Deputy Director General of Military Aeronautics;

'It is essential that these machines be replaced by something better at an early date. Will you please say when you will be able to replace these machines with FE 2bs, powered by either 160 hp Beardmore or Rolls-Royce engines, or some other type of machine.'

Indeed, both Nos 11 and 18 Sqns would replace their FB 5s with FE 2bs, but not before FB 5 5079 of No 11 Sqn was attacked by two Fokker E Is on

Right
German personnel examine the remains of FB 5 5079 of No 11 Sqn, brought down on 23 April 1916 by Ltn Max Immelmann of *FFA* 62. 2Lts William C Mortimer-Phelan and William A Scott-Brown managed to set fire to their aeroplane before being taken prisoner (*Phil Jarrett*)

23 April and driven down with a riddled petrol tank near Pelves. Its crew, 2Lts William C Mortimer-Phelan and William A Scott-Brown, were taken prisoner. Their assailants were Ltns Max Immelmann and Max *Ritter* von Mulzer of *FFA* 62, and they were credited as Immelmann's 14th victory.

Gilbert Insall's brother, Algernon J Insall, who was an observer in FB 5s, wrote retrospectively of the aeroplane in 1970;

'One came to love a machine such as the Vickers FB – perhaps because it was so fundamentally honest. It never pretended to be capable of setting speed or height records. It was quite happy bumbling along above the German Army, booming out its sonorous defiance for all to hear, and never evading a trial of strength.'

Above
An FB 5 of No 11 Sqn in flight in early 1916. For a time the Gunbus made a profound impression on the Germans, who called every armed British pusher they met a 'Vickers'. Its ascendancy was soon cut short by the advent of the Fokker E I (*Phil Jarrett*)

FIGHTING 'FEES'

In October 1914, the same month that Frantz and Quénault scored their historic aerial victory, No 6 Sqn RFC arrived in France, its flying personnel including the 23-year-old scion of a distinguished military family, Capt Lanoe George Hawker. When his unit replaced its Henry Farman F 20 pushers with BE 2cs, Hawker, like Belgian Fernand Jacquet, began to supplement his reconnaissance patrols with more aggressive activity, such as a bombing attack on Zeppelin sheds, for which he received the Distinguished Service Order (DSO).

In May 1915, No 6 Sqn began to receive FE 2b pushers to escort the BEs. The unit also acquired a single-seat Bristol Scout C for short-range frontline sorties. Compact and clean for its time, and powered by an 80 hp Gnome Lambda nine-cylinder rotary engine, the Scout embodied the biplane tractor fighter configuration that would subsequently remain standard for more than 20 years to follow.

After ferrying Scout C 1607 in from St Omer on 3 June, Hawker wrote home, 'I have a beautiful new toy – a new Bristol Scout that goes at 80 mph and climbs 500 to 600 feet a minute! I'm having a machine gun fitted to see how they like it'. The arrangement to which he referred was a Lewis mounting, devised by Air Mechanic (and future Bristol Fighter ace) Ernest J Elton, which avoided the propeller arc by firing forward, downward and outward at an angle.

In spite of the challenges of aiming such a weapon, on 21 June Hawker attacked a DFW two-seater over Poelcapelle, which was officially credited to him as 'brought down out of control' (OOC). During a forced landing the next day, Hawker overturned his 'toy', which was replaced by Scout C 1611.

During the course of three sorties on 25 June, Hawker attacked three German two-seaters. In his second combat he forced an Albatros of

An overhead view of an FE 2b engaged in its most common duty, frontline reconnaissance. The versatile pushers were also used as bombers and, in practice, if not in original intention, as two-seat fighters (*Phil Jarrett*)

Capt Lanoe G Hawker of No 6 Sqn earned fame, and the VC, for his groundbreaking actions in Bristol C scouts, but in August 1915 he added three enemy aeroplanes to his ultimate total of seven flying FE 2b 4227 (*Imperial War Museum*)

FFA 3 to land near Passchendaele at about 1845 hrs and succeeded in shooting down another in flames southeast of Zillebeke 15 minutes later, killing Oblt Alfred Uberlacker and Hptm Hans Roser, also of *FFA* 3. Hawker was credited with a double victory and subsequently received the first VC awarded for air-to-air combat.

He was no less bellicose flying his squadron's FEs, supplementing the observer's firepower with his own Lee-Enfield rifle. Flying FE 2b 4227 on 2 August, Hawker and Lt A

Payze attacked a German two-seater and forced it to land at Wulverghem. Hawker was credited with a second 'double' on 11 August, when he and Lt Noel Clifton sent an Aviatik nose-diving down to force-land near Houthem at 0545 hrs, and similarly claimed an attacking Eindecker outside Lille at 1915 that evening. Returning to Bristol Scout 1611 on 7 September, Hawker shot down an enemy biplane over Bixschoote for his seventh victory. Britain's pioneer single-seat scout pilot was now also its first ace.

It is easy, however, to overlook the fact that Hawker had scored three victories (including his ace-making fifth) not in a nimble scout, but in the most unlikely flying success story to bear the designation of 'fighter' – the two-seat FE 2b.

UNLIKELY 'ACE-MAKER'

After the first 'Farman Expermimental' FE 2 was destroyed in a crash in 1913, the Royal Aircraft Factory produced a redesign, powered by a Green engine and featuring an airbrake behind the upper wing, in February 1914. Designated the FE 2a, it was ordered into production in

Although the FE 2b's vulnerability to attack from the rear is clearly shown in this in-flight photograph, even a lone 'Fee' could put up a decent fight with a good pilot-observer team (*Phil Jarrett*)

FE 2a 5647, powered by a 120 hp Beardmore engine, bore the presentation *BOMBAY Nº 2* and flew with No 16 Sqn in November 1915. The air brake in the middle of the upper wing was dispensed with on the FE 2b (*Phil Jarrett*)

Born in Hull on 8 March 1890, 2AM David Arthur Stewart was serving with No 20 Sqn as observer to Lt D H Dabbs in FE 2d A'13 when he shot down a Fokker E III near Moorslede on 1 August 1916. Flying with Capt R S Maxwell in A'23 two days later, he downed another enemy fighter over Ypres. Subsequently qualifying as a pilot, 2Lt Stewart returned to the front flying DH 4s with No 18 Sqn and shared in 14 more victories. Promoted to captain in May 1918, he survived the war with an MC and Bar to his name (*Norman Franks*)

FE 2d A'23 became a trophy 'Vikkers Doppelecker' after being brought down by German flak on 12 May 1917. Its crew, 2Lt H Kirby and Sgt T E Wait of No 20 Sqn, became PoWs. The white No 3 on the nacelle contradicts the lack of markings that predominated in No 20 Sqn for much of the time it flew 'Fees'. On 3 August 1916, A'23, crewed by Capt Reginald Stuart Maxwell and 1AM D A Stewart, shot down a Roland C II north of Gheluwe. Born on 20 July 1894, 'George' Maxwell had downed an Aviatik on 27 April 1916 while serving with No 25 Sqn. Three more victories were to follow with No 20 Sqn, along with the awarding of an MC. Maxwell went on to add five more successes to his score flying Sopwith Camels with No 54 Sqn in 1918. Remaining in RAF service postwar, he eventually rose to the rank of air commodore in 1932 (*Aaron Weaver*)

August, and 12 were built before the Royal Aircraft Factory came out with something better. The FE 2b, powered by a 120 hp Beardmore six-cylinder engine and dispensing with the FE 2a's air brake, reached the front with No 6 Sqn in May 1915. The first all-FE 2b unit, No 20 Sqn, did not arrive in France until 16 January 1916, but eventually some 16 RFC and six Home Defence squadrons would use them.

With a wingspan of 47 ft 9 in, a length of 32 ft 3 in, a height of 12 ft 8 in, a loaded weight of 3037 lbs, a climb rate of 10,000 ft in 39 minutes and 44 seconds and a ceiling of 11,000 ft, the FE 2b neither looked nor performed – and certainly did not handle – like a fighter in the now-accepted sense of the word. Its maximum speed of 91.5 mph was faster than the FB 5's, however, and in the hands of a good crew it proved to be a tougher opponent than it looked.

The observer had a glorious field of fire for his flexibly mounted Lewis gun up front – certainly better than that of the hapless BE 2c observer, who was sat in front of the pilot amidst a maze of struts and wires, with the propeller preventing him from firing forward. However, the FE was extremely vulnerable to attack from the rear, especially when the Fokker E I appeared in mid-1915. One rather unnerving counter to that threat was the installation of a second rear-firing Lewis gun mounted on a post, which forced the observer to stand up to fire over the upper wing.

Robert Leslie Chidlaw-Roberts, who scored ten victories in SE 5as with No 60 Sqn, had previously served six months as an observer in No 2 Sqn, followed by pilot training and eight months flying FE 2bs with No 18 Sqn from 18 May to 4 December 1916. Although he scored no successes in FE 2bs, the 91-year-old survivor certainly had an opinion about them when interviewed in 1987;

'They were rather cumbersome to manouevre but the Beardmore (120 hp) engine was fairly reliable by the standards of 1916. The version with the (250 hp) Rolls-Royce engine was a much better machine, but I never flew one during my time at No 18 Sqn. We did away with the oleo undercarriage, which wasn't much good, and replaced it with a normal vee strut with rubber cord suspension.

'The poor chap in front had to jump about without a seat belt, of course, from one gun to another – it was terrible. I knew a Canadian called Rankin who fell out during a scrap. I would have hated being an observer in an FE 2b. We didn't fly very high in them, – around 8000 ft. They were good night bombers.'

Jasta 1's Hptm Martin Zander (sat in cockpit), Ltn von Carlowitz (standing second from right) and other unnamed officers pose with the remains of No 22 Sqn's A4285 after it was brought down on 25 August 1916 by Zander. Its crew, Lt Anderson and 2Lt A D Walker, were captured (*Phil Jarrett*)

One of the earliest FE 2ds issued to No 20 Sqn was A'9, which bore the legend *Presented by Residents in the PUNJAB*. It was assigned to Lt Harold E Hartney on 30 June 1916, although he scored all six of his credited 'Fee' victories in other machines (*Phil Jarrett*)

The observer to whom Chidlaw-Roberts referred, Lt F S Rankin, was participating in an escort mission for a photo-reconnaissance aeroplane on 22 October 1916 when they came under attack over Bapaume. While standing up to fire backwards, he lost his footing and fell. Fortunately for Rankin his remarkably quick-witted pilot, Lt F L Barnard, caught him by his leather jacket and hauled him back into the nacelle!

A second, necessary, adjunct toward 'Fee' survival was teamwork. When a flight of FE 2bs came under attack they would, to coin a term from Indian-fighting days on the American frontier, 'circle the wagons' in a formation that allowed the gunners to cover each other's blind spots, although Chidlaw-Roberts stated, 'I heard about it later on in the war, but we never tried it during my time in FE 2bs'. Those who did practice such tactics, however, contributed considerably to the sometimes dramatic successes that made the 'Fee' an adversary not to be underestimated. That collectivism also fostered the multiple claiming that contributed to the high scores credited to FE pilots and observers.

The Royal Aircraft Factory built 1937 FE 2bs as well as two FE 2cs, which were nightfighting and bombing variants that unsuccessfully experimented with relocating the pilot ahead of the observer. Later FE 2bs were up-powered with 160 hp Beardmores, and 386 FE 2ds were built with 275 hp Rolls-Royce Eagle engines that added 10 mph to the speed at altitudes exceeding

5000 ft and allowed them to carry greater bomb loads. According to Harold E Hartney of No 20 Sqn, some FE 2ds could also carry 'three machine guns, one of which was a pilot-fired fixed gun, but readily usable by the gunner if needed'. Although most FEs were classified as 'fighters' (the RFC used the term 'scout' for single-seaters), 395 were fitted with underwing racks to serve as bombers – a role in which, even after reaching obsolescence, they would continue to serve by night until August 1918.

'FEE' VERSUS FOKKER

FB 5s and FE 2as had encountered Fokker Eindeckers throughout the latter part of 1915, usually taking the worst of it. Having moved to Clairmarais aerodrome from St-Omer on 23 January 1916, No 20 Sqn claimed to have won the first clash between an FE 2b and a Fokker on 7 February, when Lts Guy Patrick Spencer Reid and S Billinge, escorting an RFC reconnaissance aeroplane, fired 35 rounds into an attacking Eindecker and sent it down with smoke emanating from its engine. More successes were to follow, but the squadron suffered its first of many losses on 29 February when 2Lts Lionel A Newbold and Hillary F Champion were brought down near Menin by Vzfw Wäss of *FFA* 3 and taken prisoner. Champion later escaped on 18 April and reported to RFC HQ on the 23rd.

Other squadrons were operating FE 2bs by then, but they were faring little better. On 29 March FE 2b 6352 became the 12th aeroplane credited to *FFA* 62's Oblt Max Immelmann, its crew, 2Lts F C Pinder and E A Halford of No 23 Sqn, becoming PoWs.

On 26 April 2Lts Joseph Creuss Callaghan and James Mitchell of No 18 Sqn were on a photo-reconnaissance mission in FE 2b 5232 when they were attacked by three Fokkers of *FFA* 62 over Souchez. In a spirited fight, the FE crew claimed an attacker – although the Germans suffered no casualties – before crossing the lines, where Callaghan, his controls damaged, turned upside down before landing near Château de la Haie.

FE 2b 6356 of No 20 Sqn was brought down on the road between Marguillies and Sainghin on 9 March 1916, 2Lts Leo Roy Haywood and Douglas Byron Gayford becoming PoWs. Observer Gayford claimed to have destroyed an LVG (actually Albatros C I 1833/15 of *FFA* 18, killing Ltns Gerhardt *Freiherr* von Gayl and Erwin Friedel) before his Lewis gun jammed and he was attacked by two Fokkers from *FFA* 5. One of the German pilots fired 200 rounds and wound Gayford four times, before a hit in the radiator drove the 'Fee' to ground. Haywood was also wounded in the foot by enemy fire (*Greg VanWyngarden*)

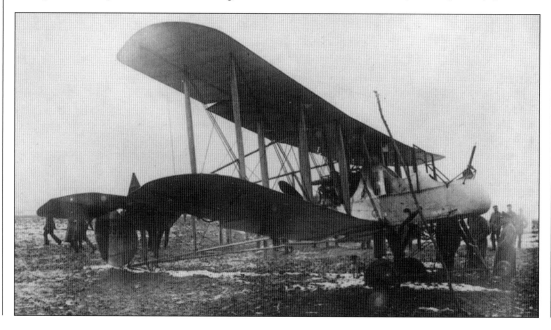

German troops recover FE 2b 6341, bearing the legend *Presented by the Government of ZANZIBAR Nº 1* on one side of its nacelle and *THE SCOTCH EXPRESS* on the other, along with the single black band of 'A' Flight, No 25 Sqn. The aircraft was brought down on 16 May 1916, and its crew, Capt Douglas Grinnell-Milne and Cpl D MacMaster, were made PoWs (*Jon Guttman*)

Oblt Max Immelmann was one of the first German fighter pilots to capture the public's imagination – and the first of many German aces to fall victim to an FE 2b, although the outcome of the encounter of 18 June 1916 is still debated (*Imperial War Museum Q45328*)

German troops pose soberly before FE 2b 4909 *BABY MINE*, which bears two yellow(?) bands denoting its assignment to 'B' Flight of No 25 Sqn, after it was brought down near Noyelles on 18 June 1916. Its pilot, Lt John R B Savage, died from his wounds, and the wounded observer, 2Lt T N U Robinson, was captured. Arriving too late to help their flightmates, 2Lt G R McCubbin and Cpl J H Waller in FE 2b 6346 nevertheless claimed one of the two attackers, who turned out to be Oblt Max Immelmann of *FFA* 62. Immelmann's wingman, Ltn Max Mulzer, took credit for 4909 (*Greg VanWyngarden*)

Once on the ground, he discovered that Mitchell had died from a head wound. Callaghan, an Irishman who had resided in Texas before the outbreak of war drew him back to join the Royal Munster Fusiliers and subsequently the RFC, was awarded the MC for this action. In January 1918 he would command No 87 Sqn and score four more victories in Sopwith Dolphins, before being shot down and killed on 2 July by Ltn Franz Büchner of *Jasta* 13.

In spite of the claims they put in, the FE 2b crews were not inflicting casualties on the *Eindeckerflieger* commensurate with their own, although the attrition they endured was far less than that suffered by the BE 2s, which had by then acquired the lamentable sobriquet of 'Fokker Fodder'. The 'Fee's' rep-

SIEGER

ENGL. DOPPELDECKER ABGESCHOSSEN
16.5.16 bei FOURNES

utation became considerably fiercer on the evening of 18 June, when four Fokkers of *FFA* 62 sallied forth from their aerodrome at Doaui to intercept seven FE 2bs of No 25 Sqn. Oblt Immelmann, in Fokker E III 246/16, attacked FE 2b 4909, which came down near Lens, where the pilot, 17-year-old Lt John R B Savage, died of his wounds and observer 2AM T N U Robinson was taken prisoner.

Flying at a higher altitude in FE 2b 6346, 2Lt G R McCubbin, from Cape Town, South Africa, saw Savage's plight and dived to his aid, pursued by two other Fokkers. In 1935 he described what happened;

'Savage's machine suddenly went out of control, as the Fokker had been firing at it, and Savage's machine went down. By this time I was very close to the Fokker, and he apparently realised we were on his tail as he immediately started to do what I expect was the beginning of an "Immelmann" turn. As he started the turn we opened fire and the Fokker immediately went out of control and fell down to earth'.

Crashing near Sallaumines from 2000 ft, Germany's first fighter hero Max Immelmann, 'The Eagle of Lille', was dead. Savage and Robinson were not counted among his 15 victories, instead being claimed by and credited to his wingman, Ltn Max von Mülzer. Once the British learned of Immelmann's demise they awarded the DSO to McCubbin, while his observer, Cpl J H Waller, got the DSM and a promotion to sergeant. The Germans attributed Immelmann's loss to a malfunction of the machine gun's synchronisation system, resulting in him shooting his own propeller off, but Waller retrospectively asserted that 'it is quite on the cards that our bullets not only got him, but his

A German composite photograph of FE 2b 6341 (also seen on the previous page) and the Fokker E III of Vzfw Adam Barth of *FFA* 18, to whom it was credited. After the war, Capt Douglas Grinnell-Milne stated that four Fokker E IIIs had 'ganged up' on his aeroplane, one of which his observer sent down to crash before a ruptured petrol tank in turn forced them to land (*Greg VanWyngarden*)

This photograph of the wreckage of an unidentified FE 2d was taken from a German soldier killed in the trenches on 29 October 1917. The image was subsequently published in the *Daily Despatch* (*Phil Jarrett*)

prop as well, and that would be the reason for them trying to make this statement.'

It was not to be the last time an ace would fall casualty to a ponderous 'Fee', nor the last time that such a loss would be attended by controversy. Meanwhile, a new pusher design had reached France to answer the enemy's challenge for aerial supremacy – this time a single-seater.

FE 2b 5206 from No 20 Sqn's 'B' Flight was brought down near Houthem on 21 May 1916 as the fifth victory for Vfw Wilhelm Frankl of *FFA* 40. Capt Charles Ernest Hilton James and 2Lt Henry Leslie Cautley Aked were made PoWs (*Greg VanWyngarden*)

Typifying unit and flight markings for No 11 Sqn is FE 2b 7691 of 'B' Flight, photographed after it was shot down on 31 March 1917 by Ltn Kurt Wolff of *Jasta* 11 (*Greg VanWyngarden*)

German troops examine the nacelle of FE 2b 7691, which they had tipped onto its nose in order to extricate the stricken observer, 2Lt W G T Clifton, who subsequently died of his wounds. The pilot, 2Lt L A T Strange, was made a PoW. This machine was yet another presentation aircraft, as proclaimed by the extensive titling on the nacelle (*Greg VanWyngarden*)

SINGLE-SEAT PUSHERS

Posted back to England soon after achieving 'acedom', on 28 September 1915 Capt Lanoe G Hawker was sent to Hownslow to take command of the RFC's first single-seat fighter unit. No 24 Sqn's equipment, the Airco DH 2, represented yet another early method for a machine gun-armed single-seater to circumvent the propeller – this time in the hands of just one rather busy pilot.

After leaving the Royal Aircraft Factory to join the Aircraft Manufacturing Co Ltd in June 1914, Geoffrey de Havilland had designed the Airco DH 1, which was a two-seat pusher of similar configuration to the FE 2. In the early summer of 1915 he introduced a more compact single-seat version, the DH 2, which reached a speed of 93 mph and climbed at a rate of 545 ft per minute. Soon after its first flight in July 1915, the prototype (4732) was sent to France for operational evaluation.

The new scout's frontline debut could scarcely have been less promising. Upon its arrival in France on 26 July, 4732's 100 hp Gnome monosoupape rotary engine had to be replaced. The aeroplane was then attached to No 5 Sqn, but disappeared over enemy lines on 9 August. The Germans subsequently dropped a message stating that the DH 2's pilot, Captain R Maxwell-Pike, had died of his injuries, and a photograph showed that the pusher had flipped over onto its back upon landing, but was otherwise intact. Although presented with a near-

Below and bottom
On 26 July 1915, prototype Airco DH 2 4732 was sent to No 5 Sqn in France for operational evaluation, where it was lost on 9 August. The Germans, who informed the British that the scout's pilot, Capt R Maxwell-Pike, had died of his injuries, photographed the aeroplane and recovered it for evaluation. Despite having intimate knowledge of the aircraft prior to it even entering squadron service with the RFC, German pilots would continue to misidentify DH 2s as 'Vickers scouts' with curious regularity (*Aaron Weaver and Greg Van Wyngarden*)

perfect advance glimpse at Britain's latest fighter, for more than a year thereafter German aviators kept misidentifying DH 2s as 'Vickers scouts' with curious regularity.

In spite of the disastrous loss of the prototype, Airco put the DH 2 into production. The next two examples were delivered to Nos 11 and 18 Sqns in January 1916, and eventually 453 DH 2s were built.

Back in Britain, No 24 Sqn got its first DH 2 on 10 January, and its strength was up to 12 when it moved to Bertangles, in France, on 10 February. The newly promoted Maj Hawker discovered that there was work to be done before his

DH 2 prototype 4732's nacelle minus its fabric. Note how close the pilot sat to the fuel tank (*Aaron Weaver*)

squadron was ready to take on the 'Fokker Scourge', but as a former sapper he was perpetually ready to reach for the tools whenever there was a problem to solve.

In its original form, the DH 2 carried a Lewis gun with a 47-round magazine in a fairing on the port side of the pilot's nacelle. The production version placed the gun centrally in the front of the nacelle on a vertical shaft that gave it considerable range of movement. Hawker thought this 'wobbly mounting', which required the pilot to fly the aircraft with one hand and aim his weapon with the other, useless, and clamped the gun in a forward firing position. Higher authorities prohibited such practice, but Hawker compromised by devising a spring clip that would theoretically allow the pilot to release the gun for flexible use. In practice, Hawker's men almost never unclipped their guns in combat.

Besides turning the DH 2 into a more stable gun platform, Hawker devised a ring sight for the gun and an 'aiming off model' – a device to make allowances for high-speed movement. He also came up with the 'rocking fuselage' training aid, which was built under his supervision in the squadron workshop so that pilots could practice their aerial marksmanship at targets sat alongside a railway embankment. Although one excessively rocking fuselage resulted in the telegraph wires alongside the embankment being shot through – bringing GHQ's wrath upon Hawker – his 'gadget' ultimately gained universal acceptance.

The rear-mounted rotary engine near its centre of gravity made the DH 2 highly manoeuvrable, but it also meant that the fighter had a disconcerting propensity to fall into a spin, which caused a number of training accidents. Little was known about how to recover from a spin at the time, but Hawker understood the concept of centralising the controls.

After hearing his pilots speak of the DH 2's spinning tendencies in February 1916, Hawker wordlessly left the squadron mess, took an aeroplane up to 8000 ft, deliberately put it into a spin and then pulled out of it. He repeated the performance several times, from right and left handed turns, then landed and rejoined his men in the mess. 'It's all right you fellows', he announced. 'You can get the DH 2 out of any spin. I have

In the course of preparing No 24 Sqn and its DH 2s for battle, Maj Lanoe G Hawker VC came up with technical and tactical innovations that well earned him his reputation as 'the English Boelcke' (*Jon Guttman*)

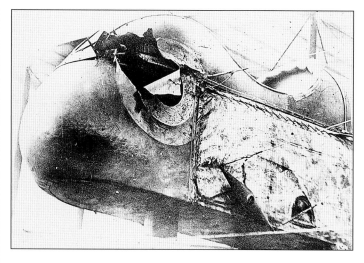

The nacelle of DH 2 5924 after a shell passed through it on 21 April 1916. Miraculously, pilot 2Lt David Mary Tidmarsh, who had scored No 24 Sqn's first victory in this aeroplane on 2 April, was unharmed (*Greg VanWyngarden*)

Another founding member of No 24 Sqn, and future ace, Capt John Oliver Andrews is seen here wearing the hat of his former unit, the Royal Scots Regiment. He scored seven of his 12 victories in DH 2s, five in 5998 (*Aaron Weaver*)

just tried it out'. His men promptly practiced at his technique and No 24 Sqn had no further spinning-related accidents.

Yet another problem afflicting the DH 2 was expressed by then-Flt Sgt James Thomas Byford McCudden of No 29 Sqn;

'The DH 2 was a very cold machine, as the pilot had to sit in a small nacelle with the engine a long way back, and so of course he got no warmth from it at all.'

Hawker addressed that problem too by designing fleece-lined flying clothes, including the hip-high 'fug boots' that would become popular among British airmen – and German airmen fortunate enough to capture any – throughout the war.

Once its personnel had gained sufficient experience and confidence, No 24 Sqn fought its first aerial engagement on 19 March. A new setback occurred on the six days later, however, when a strong westerly wind drove one of the unit's DH 2s down in German lines, thus presenting the enemy with another, this time completely intact, specimen.

On 2 April 2Lt David Marie Tidmarsh, a resident of Limerick who had served with the 4th Regiment, Irish Special Reserve, before transferring into the RFC, and Lt S J Sibley officially opened No 24 Sqn's account when they shot an Albatros down between Grandcourt and Albert, killing Uffz Paul Wein and Ltn d R Karl Oskar Breibisch-Guthmann of *FFA* 32. Tidmarsh had a close call on the 21st, when an anti-aircraft shell went through the nacelle of his DH 2 (5924) without exploding or wounding him.

On 25 April three of No 24's DH 2s were escorting a BE 2c of No 15 Sqn when they were attacked by a flight of Fokkers. The pushers turned on the enemy, drove down one of the Eindeckers and chased off the rest. Their victim was probably leading ace Max Immelmann, who wrote of his 'nasty fight' that day;

'I took off at about 1100 hrs and met two English biplanes south of Bapaume. I was about 700 metres lower than them, and therefore came up and attacked one. He seemed to heel over after a few shots, but unfortunately I was mistaken. The two worked splendidly together in the course of the fight and put 11 shots in my machine. The petrol tank, the struts on the fuselage, the undercarriage and the propeller were hit. I could only save myself by a nose-dive of 1000 metres.'

The men who Immelmann thought worked so 'splendidly together' were Lts N P Manfield and John Oliver Andrews. The latter, born on 20 July 1890 in Waterloo, Lancashire, had served in the Royal Scottish Regiment before taking to the air as an observer in Avro 504s with No 5 Sqn. He later took flight training at Le Crotoy, in France, qualifying as a pilot on 19 October 1915 and re-entering combat with No 24 Sqn.

The 25 April action sealed the DH 2 pilots' confidence in their mounts, and from then on they attacked all German aircraft they

encountered without hesitation. While Immelmann had been merely chastened by his encounter with No 24 Sqn, another scrap on the 30th turned out far worse for Ltn Otto Schmedes of *Kampfeinsitzer Kommando* (*KEK*) Bertincourt, attached to *FFA* 32. 2Lt Tidmarsh, flying DH 2 5965, was escorting some FEs over Péronne when he spotted an approaching Eindecker and attacked it. The German dived, but seemed to lose control at an altitude of 1000 ft, after which the wings separated and he crashed into some houses at Bapaume.

The German report of Schmedes' death stated that his flying wires had been severed by bullets, but Tidmarsh claimed he never got closer than 500 yards and did not have the opportunity to fire. Those inconsistencies notwithstanding, Tidmarsh was credited with the Fokker. On 20 May he teamed up with Capt W A Summers of No 22 Sqn to despatch a two-seater in flames south of Pozières, probably killing the *FFA* 32 crew of Gefr Franz Patzig and Ltn d R Georg Lönholdt.

Tidmarsh did no further scoring in DH 2s, but after taking leave in England he returned to the front in March 1917 as a flight leader in No 48 Sqn, flying the new Bristol F 2A two-seat fighter. He was credited with victories on 8 and 10 April and two Albatros D IIIs on the 11th, but during the course of that last fight he and his observer, 2 Lt C B Holland, were brought down by Ltn Kurt Wolff of *Jasta* 11, and he spent the rest of the war as a PoW.

While No 24 Sqn was establishing the DH 2 as a force to be reckoned with, No 29 Sqn began arriving at St-Omer on 25 March, although it then moved to Abeele on 15 April. One of its members, future 32-victory ace 2Lt Geoffrey Hilton Bowman, summed up its initial operations. 'Nothing much happened in No 29 Sqn during 1916. We were in the Ypres salient and all the Huns had gone down to the Somme'.

On 4 June No 32 Sqn, commanded by FB 5 ace Maj L W B Rees, joined No 25 Sqn at St Auchel. Like Hawker, Rees, who had published a booklet on how to rig the DH 2, did all he could to train his pilots on the

Seen at Hounslow in January 1916, these brand new DH 2s, and a solitary Bristol M I, were all assigned to No 24 Sqn. The unit transferred to France early the following month (*Aaron Weaver*)

Lt Muir of No 24 Sqn waits for the signal to take off in a DH 2 fitted with an external rack to give him quicker access to extra Lewis machine gun magazines (*Greg VanWyngarden*)

scout. On 9 May 2Lt Gwilym Hugh Lewis, a fellow Welshman in No 32 Sqn, had written of Rees, 'He knows his job thoroughly and above all is a perfect gentleman. I shouldn't be surprised if he comes home with a VC – he has already got an MC'.

That night, the 18-year-old Lewis cockily wrote home about the 'respect' that his aeroplane had already acquired;

'The DH 2 has pratially scared the Huns off the Front. Occasionally, they manage to steal over at 15,000 ft, but even then they hesitate as to whether they should dive on a DH or not, even if it happens to be below them. The FEs complain that they can get hardly any fights now – it is awfully amusing. Of course, the DH pilot's job is to attack, and away he goes at any Hun he sees. Personally, I am less scared of attacking a single-seater Fokker than a slower two-seater with a couple of gun mountings'.

On 7 June No 32 Sqn moved to Treizennes and familiarised itself with the sector. It was about to join No 24 Sqn in support of Gen Sir Douglas Haig's great ground offensive along the River Somme.

BATTLE OF THE SOMME

When the Somme offensive commenced on 1 July, the sheer number of British reconnaissance, artillery spotter and bombing aircraft assured the RFC a measure of aerial supremacy, but the German fighters struck regularly under conditions of their choosing in an often effective effort to disrupt Allied air operations. Among the units seeking to counter the enemy scouts were the DH 2s of Nos 24 and 32 Sqns, joined by No 60 Sqn and its Morane-Saulnier N tractor monoplanes that employed the same bullet deflectors used by Roland Garros back in April 1915.

The night before the 'Big Push', Maj Hawker had issued a simple directive to his pilots – 'Tactical Orders OC No 24 Sqn. Attack everything'. The man who best followed that order was Dublin-born 2Lt Sidney Edward Cowan, who claimed two two-seaters near Pys at 0745 hrs (one of which one was credited as OOC) for his second victory of an eventual seven.

It was No 32 Sqn's Maj Rees, however, who set the most noteworthy example for his men on 1 July. He and Canadian-born Lt J C Simpson took off at 0555 hrs, with the latter pilot patrolling the area around La Bassée, Loos and Souchez, while Rees skirted the line awaiting the return of a bombing flight and its DH 2 escorts. Simpson spotted ten Roland and Albatros two-seaters of *Kagohl 3*'s *Kasta* 14 on a bombing mission of their own and attacked. However, a fusillade from three of the Germans sent him crashing into the Loos Canal with eight bullets in his head.

Capt Herman W von Poellnitz takes off from Vert Galand aerodrome in July 1916. Just visible are 'B' Flight markings on the wheel hubs, while the strut streamers indicate von Poelnitz's flight leader status (*Phil Jarrett*)

Born in Downpatrick, Ireland, on 23 August 1897, Lt Sidney Edward Cowan was a founder member of No 24 Sqn when it formed at Hounslow around a nucleus of personnel drawn from No 17 Sqn on 1 September 1915. He subsequently scored six victories with the unit between 4 May and 16 September, earning the MC and Bar. Transferring to command 'C' Flight of No 29 Sqn, Capt Cowan downed a Halberstadt D II OOC on 17 November, but as he went after another German aircraft his DH 2 (A2555) collided with 2Lt W S F Saundby's A2565 and both men were killed (*Norman Franks*)

Moments later Rees sighted the German formation, which he at first thought was British. As he approached it, however, one aeroplane dived at him, firing. Responding with 30 rounds of his own, Rees reported that he 'saw the top of the fuselage splinter between the pilot and observer', and the enemy aircraft dived away to the east.

At that point Rees attacked a lone Roland, and three others rushed to its aid. While the latter fired at a hopelessly long range, Rees emptied a drum into his quarry. He subsequently wrote, 'After about 30 rounds, a big cloud of blue haze came out of the nacelle in front of the pilot'.

As that aeroplane fled over the lines, Rees attacked five more Germans. Gwilym Lewis, who thought Rees 'the bravest man in the world', described what ensued;

'The Huns were in a tight bunch when he came along – after he had finished they were scattered in twos and ones all over the sky, not knowing which way to go. He sent the first one down out of control, and the second one probably had a bullet through his engine. He turned to attack the third, whose observer was sitting with his head back and his gun aiming vertically upwards, fairly blazing off bullets. I suppose he must have forgotten to take his hand off the trigger before he "pipped out". Just as the Major was going to get this machine as a trophy, another fellow came and shot him in the leg from below. He was still going on, but when he discovered that he couldn't steer his machine he came home.'

Although he had suffered temporary paralysis, Rees regained some use of his leg and turned to pursue the German leader, which after dropping a bomb was making for its own lines. Expending a full drum and even drawing his pistol, only to drop it into the nacelle, Rees finally gave up as the two-seater was too far away and too high. As it was, he had scattered the German bombing formation, and the observer he had hit in the third aeroplane – mortally, it turned out – was Ltn Erich Zimmermann, commander of *Kasta*14, whose wounded pilot, Ltn d R Ernst Wendler, crash-landed near La Bassée.

'He landed in the usual manner and taxied in', Lewis wrote. 'They got the steps for him to get out of his machine. He got out and sat on the grass, at which point he calmly told the fellows to bring him a tender to take him to hospital. I am afraid to report that he has suffered a very bad wound, although he is lucky not to have had an artery in his leg shot, as I understand that he would never have got back if he had.'

Joining the RFC on 10 August 1914, Capt Lionel Wilmot Brabazon B Rees teamed up with Flt Sgt J M Hargreaves to score five victories between 28 July and 30 September 1915. These successes made them the only Vickers FB 5 aces of the war. Rees downed a sixth opponent (an LVG) in collaboration with Flt Sgt Raymond on 31 October. He gained further distinction as commander of No 32 Sqn, and was awarded a VC for his leadership of the unit in action on 1 July 1916 (*Greg VanWyngarden*)

DH 2s of No 32 Sqn line up at Vert Galand farm in late July 1916. The unit had moved here from Treizennes on the 21st of the month. At right, standing between two pilots ready for take-off, is Maj Tom Alger Elliott Cairnes, who took command of the unit after Maj Rees was wounded (*Aaron Weaver*)

'Of course, everyone knows the Major is mad. I don't think he was ever more happy in his life than attacking those Huns. He said he would have brought them all down one after the other if he could have used his leg.'

Rees was credited with a Roland OOC and one 'forced to land', raising his total to eight. He duly received the VC for exploits during this mission. Rees spent the rest of the war commanding the Air Fighting School at Ayr, and remained in RAF service until 1931, when he retired as a group captain. He died in the Bahamas on 28 September 1955.

The Somme's first day also saw five No 20 Sqn FEs fighting off 20 Fokkers over Armentières and claiming five of them, including two crashed, even though the Germans recorded no pilot losses. Lt Guy Reid, formerly of the Seaforth Highlanders, was credited with one in FE 2b A'11, as was his observer, Capt G Dixon-Spain. Two others were credited as OOC to Lt Hartney and 2AM A Stanley in new FE 2d A'3.

Born in Pakenham, Ontario on 19 April 1888, Harold Evans Hartney had been mobilised in October 1914. Married just before he shipped out to England in May 1915, he transferred to the RFC in October. Reporting to No 20 Sqn at Clairmarais on 16 June, he flew his first sortie over the lines on the 30th. Now, on Canada's Dominion Day, he found himself above the British Expeditionary Force's greatest offensive to date. Looking up, he spotted a diving Fokker E III firing bullets down on him.

'Frightened out of my wits, I leaned over and hit Stanley a vicious clout on the head', Hartney wrote, 'and then I had my first real lesson in aerial acrobatics. Holding the left wing slightly depressed, I slammed my foot down on the right-hand rudder. I thought that the big aeroplane would tear itself to pieces as the resulting side-slip skidded us downward to the left in a wild partial corskscrew lurch. All I could see of Stanley was his hand in front of me, clinging tensely to the nacelle ring. Now the other wing down, stick back, nose slightly up and a momentary kick on the opposite rudder. A quick glance, both sides – no sign of the Hun, so I got ready for a gamble and a blind Immelmann.

'Swiftly, after a short preliminary straightaway dive, I leaned forcibly back on the stick. Then, as all controls became flabby and we were poised momentarily in the air, crash with the right foot down on the rudder and

No 32 Sqn in July 1916. These pilots are, from left to right, Lts G H Bonnell, Inman, M J Maremontenboult and F H Coleman, Capt J M Robb, Lt L P Aizlewood, Capt H W G Jones, R H Wallace, Capts Nicholas, E Henty and G N Martin, Maj T A E Cairnes, Capts G Allen, Charles Bath, H W von Poellnitz, O V Thomas, G H Lewis and B P G Hunt (*Phil Jarrett*)

in a split second, out of control, we reversed direction. Now we were headed back for enemy territory again in complete control. And there, right in front of me, streaking like hell, and slightly below us, was my German friend.'

Stanley fired five four-shot bursts at the oncoming enemy. 'His tank ablaze, he pulled up almost directly in front of us', Hartney recalled, 'then whip-stalled to Eternity'.

Now separated from their formation and deep behind enemy lines, Hartney headed back, fighting his way through what Stanley believed was 11 'scraps' (during three of which his gun jammed) with enemy fighters, attacking from fore and aft. On one occasion a Fokker retired from its firing pass along a straight route and Hartney turned onto its tail. 'With my superior speed and Stanley's cool judgment and skillful aim', Hartney wrote, 'another German ship went hurling earthward – not in the familiar unguided spin but in a straight dive, smoke streaking out behind him'.

Ultimately, with one of Stanley's guns jammed and the other out of ammunition, Hartney made it to the frontlines and carried out a forced landing in a stretch of ploughed ground behind the Australian trenches. 'Then we began to inspect our aeroplane', recalled the Canadian. 'It was in horrible shape, riddled with bullets. How it held together is a mystery.

'The fabric in places was torn clear from the leading edge to the trailing. The motor should have been put in a museum, as seven bullets were actually sticking in the water jackets and the plumbing and the cowling was almost a sieve. And that is the gospel truth, although my word on it has often been doubted – four of the aluminium pistons, a secret Rolls-Royce innovation, had actually fused and were holding up four of the exhaust valves. There was no water whatsoever in the engine and practically no oil. For those last few minutes it had been doing its bit for old England metal to metal at melting temperatures.'

YANKS IN THE RAF

During the summer of 1916, a growing amount of attention was falling on a French squadron comprised of volunteers from the neutral United States that was operating over the Verdun sector. By the end of the year this unit, N124, would coin a term for itself that would endow it with worldwide renown – the *Escadrille Lafayette*.

Completely overlooked (and quite content to be) amid all the publicity that this outfit would generate was a contingent of Americans who had made their way into the RFC or Royal Naval Air Service (RNAS), sometimes under Canadian guise. Among them was Lt Geoffrey H Bonnell, who flew DH 2s with No 32 Sqn and later went on to command the 147th Aero Squadron of the 1st Pursuit Group, US Army Air Service (USAS), in 1918.

Also making his debut during the offensive was Lt Frederick Libby, a cowboy from Sterling, Colorado, who was riding cattle in Canada when the war broke out. He joined the army there in 1915, and after some time in the trenches he transferred to the RFC as an observer with No 23 Sqn. Libby noted this first impression of the FE 2b;

'The pilot is in front of the motor in the middle of the ship and the observer in front of the pilot. When you stand, all of you from the knees up is exposed to the world. There is no belt and nothing to hold on to except

Coloradan Frederick Libby had been a cowboy before he enlisted in Canada and became an FE 2b observer in No 23 Sqn, downing an Ago on his first mission on 15 July 1916. He and Lt Stephen Price later transferred to No 11 Sqn, where they teamed up for seven of Libby's nine credited victories with that unit. Subsequently training as a pilot, Libby added two to his score flying Sopwith 1½ Strutters with No 43 Sqn and two more in DH 4s with No 25 Sqn. He died in Los Angeles, California, on 6 January 1970, aged 79 (*Sally Ann Marsh*)

the gun and sides of the nacelle. Fastened to the bottom and toward the front of the nacelle is a hollow steel rod with a specially mounted swivel mount for anchoring the machine gun, which can be swung from side to side or to the front as the occasion demands, giving it a wonderful field of fire.

'Between the observer and the pilot is another gun, which is for the purpose of fighting a rear-guard action over the top wing to protect your tail. The mounting consists of a hollow steel rod, into which a solid steel rod is fitted to work up and down with the machine gun on

Lt Geoffrey H Bonnell, who was an American volunteer in No 32 Sqn, sits in the nacelle of a DH 2. Bonnell would later join the USAS and command the 147th Aero Squadron (*Phil Jarrett*)

top. To operate this you simply pull the gun up as high as possible, where it locks into the fitting, then you step out of the nacelle and stand with a foot on each side. From this position you have nothing to worry about except being blown out of the ship or being tossed out if the pilot makes a wrong move. This gun, I know, I am not going to like much.'

One of the squadron's sergeants, noting Libby's outstanding marksmanship during early gunnery exercises, briefed him on the missions, and his place in them;

'You know, Libby, all FE 2b squadrons are all-purpose squadrons. While being primarily a fighting squadron, they can do anything, such as reconnaissance or bombing, and while the Hun is faster and more manoeuvrable, the FE 2b in the hands of a good pilot and observer is hard to defeat. In fact, it is so solid that unless they hit the pilot or engine, the ship will keep afloat and limp home, often riddled with bullets, and here is where you come in.

No 32 Sqn DH 2 7907, which features flight colours on its wheel hubs (*Phil Jarrett*)

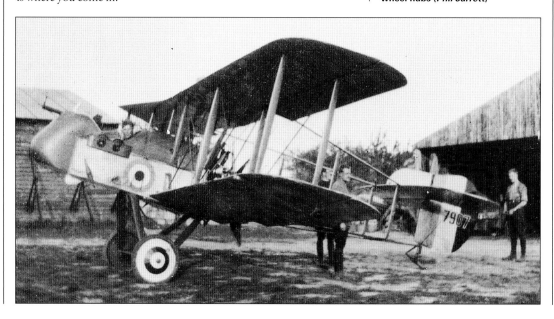

'The observer is the most essential part of the team. You do all the shooting, all the photography, all the bomb dropping, if bombs are used. And you're entirely responsible for your pilot's life. True, the pilot flies the ship. He gets you there and back, and a good pilot will put you in a position to shoot and will not get panicky, tossing the ship around, throwing you out of position to shoot or defend yourself.'

'As for our FE 2b', said Lt E D Hicks, Libby's first assigned pilot, 'the enemy have a wholesome respect for it. A good observer can shoot from any angle, and it has a wonderful range of vision with the front gun. The rear gun is to keep "Fritz" off your tail when returning home from across the lines, when you can't turn and fight with the front gun unless forced to. If this happens, you lose your formation back of the lines and have to fight your way home alone. This is tough, and is just what the Hun is after. A lone ship they all jump on, so we try to keep formation at any cost if possible. Fighting your way home in a single ship, the odds are all in favour of your enemy. The wind is almost always against you because it blows from the west off the sea – this they know and they can wait.'

Flying with Hicks as his pilot on 15 July, Fred Libby (who turned 24 that very day) credited with an Ago C I destroyed in flames over Bapaume, shared with the crew of Lt Tyler and 2Lt J A Turnbull. Soon afterwards, Libby was assigned to Lt Stephen William Price, and both men were transferred to No 11 Sqn. Here, Price took command of 'B' Flight. On 22 August the duo, flying FE 2b 6994, were credited with three Rolands south of Bapaume – two were shared with 2Lt Lionel B F Morris and Lt Tom Rees in 6983. An Aviatik on the 25th and a two-seater on 14 September (both achieved with Price as his pilot) made Libby the first American ace of the war, although the first American *pilot* to attain that status would be Adj Raoul Lufbery of N124 on 12 October.

No 24 Sqn was equally active throughout the Somme offensive. At 0800 hrs on 21 July, a patrol led by Capt Andrews took on five Roland C IIs, escorted by five Fokkers, near Roisel. During the course of the scrap Andrews shot down an Eindecker at Allaines, which Lt S E Pither also fired at as it descended. Andrews reported seeing the Fokker smash its undercarriage in a forced landing, and he subsequently fired on, and scattered, a group of Germans approaching the wreck.

'Jock' Andrews' first confirmed victory was most likely Ltn Otto Parschau, an eight-victory ace and recent recipient of the *Orden Pour le Mérite*, who was struck in the chest and head and died of his wounds soon after. Ltn Werner Schramm of *FFA* 32 and Vzfw Wolfgang Heinemann of *FFA* 62 were also killed on 21 July 1916, making this the worst day of loss for the Eindecker pilots.

Another Fokker was credited as OOC on 31 July to Lt Robert Henry Magnus Spencer Saundby, a former member of the Royal Warwickshire Regiment who had joined the RFC in January 1916 and been among No 24 Sqn's original complement. This was the first success in what would prove to be a rather circuitous route to 'acedom' for the 20-year-old Saundby.

Born on 28 November 1895, Stephen William Price came from Woodside Park, London, and served in the 8th Leicestershire Regiment prior to qualifying as a pilot at Ruislip on 27 October 1915. He subsequently served in Nos 23, 11, 33 (Home Defence) and 36 (HD) Sqns, scoring seven victories while flying FE 2bs with No 11 between August and October 1916 (*Norman Franks*)

NEW OPPOSITION

For all the RFC's efforts, the Battle of the Somme fell disappointingly short of being the decisive breakthrough Haig had expected. The British

suffered some 60,000 casualties on the first day, and tens of thousands more died on both sides in the weeks that followed for little or no substantial gain.

In the air, the DH 2 had effectively put paid to the 'Fokker Scourge', but that achievement, too, would soon become irrelevant. On 22 June the first Halberstadt D I biplane had arrived at Douai aerodrome. By the 29th there were eight at the front. One, flown by Ltn Gustav Leffers of *FFA 32*, shot down an FE 2b of No 11 Sqn over Miraumont on 9 July.

Even as the Halberstadts proliferated, Germany's first specialised fighter squadrons, or *Jagdstaffeln*, began to form. *Jasta* 2, organised on 27 August under the command of Hptm Oswald Boelcke, was initially equipped with two Fokker biplanes and the first frontline example of another new fighter type, the Albatros D I.

Designed by Robert Thelen, the D I was a single-seat single-bay biplane with a streamlined plywood fuselage, powered by a neatly cowled 160 hp Mercedes D III engine driving a propeller that boasted a spinner. Just as formidable as its horsepower was its firepower – not one, but two synchronised 7.92 mm Parabellum 08/14 machine guns.

Although German airmen agreed that the Albatros' superior speed and rate of fire offset most Allied fighters' ability to outmanoeuvre it, they complained that its upper wing and trestle-type centre section struts impeded their upward vision. Thelen responded by lowering the upper wing and supporting it with outward-splayed N-shaped cabane struts on the Albatros D II. He also replaced the drag-producing 'ear' type Windhoff radiators on the fuselage sides of the D I and early D II with a Teeves und Braun radiator installed flush in the upper wing centre section. One of *Jasta* 2's earliest members, and future ace, Ltn Erwin Böhme wrote of the Albatros fighters, 'With them, one can dare and achieve anything'.

Boelcke scored *Jasta* 2's first victory in a Fokker D III, bringing down a DH 2 of No 32 Sqn north of Thiepval on 2 September, after which he cordially showed its uninjured pilot, Capt R E Wilson, around his

Capt Price and Lt Libby fly over Bapaume in an FE 2b with a repaired right upper wing on 23 September 1916. Libby had scored his seventh victory (an unidentified scout OOC) with Sgt Thompson as his pilot 24 hours earlier (*Sally Ann Marsh*)

Born in Eastbourne, Sussex, on 21 November 1891, Oxford-educated Alan Machin Wilkinson scored ten victories in the DH 2 with No 24 Sqn, before pioneering the possibilities of the Bristol F 2 Fighter with No 48 Sqn by claiming nine more victories during 'Bloody April' 1917 (*Norman Franks*)

aerodrome at Bertincourt, before sending him off to a PoW camp! On the same day Lt Patrick Anthony Langan-Byrne, a 21-year-old Irish member of No 24 Sqn from Clopherhead, County Leith, claimed a German fighter OOC just 72 hours after having scored his first victory, and Capt Andrews destroyed a single-seater north of Les Boeufs for his third success. On the 6th Andrews and Saundby teamed up to bring down a two-seater east of Flers.

Boelcke continued to fly Fokker and Halberstadt scouts over the next two weeks, adding six more Allied aircraft to his score. One was flown by 'Jock' Andrews' squadronmate, Lt Manfield, who was killed over Thiepval in a DH 2 on 9 September. Another was DH 2 7873 flown by 2Lt J V Bowring of 'C' Flight, which was brought down on the 14th. Although wounded, Bowring survived the incident as a PoW. The following day Lt Langan-Byrne claimed an enemy scout in flames northeast of Morval.

On 16 September *Jasta* 2 finally received a substantial complement of five Albatros D Is and one D II. Later that same afternoon, Ltn Otto Walter Höhne scored the first victory in a D I when he downed an FE 2b of No 11 Sqn, whose crew was taken prisoner.

Twenty-four hours later Boelcke inaugurated an innovation more significant than the Albatros – a team effort at gaining local air superiority. At 1300 hrs he led five of his men toward British lines, where he spotted 14 British aircraft heading for Marcoing railway station. Boelcke led his formation to intercept them, but the British reached their target first and were bombing the station when the Germans arrived. While Boelcke held back, five of his men dived on the bombers and their escorts, broke up the formations and then went after lone targets. In the next five minutes three FE 2bs of No 11 Sqn fell to Boelcke, Ltn d R Hans Reimann and Ltn Manfred *Freiherr* von Richthofen. The latter's first success resulted in the deaths of 2Lt L B F Morris and Tom Rees, whose captaincy had just been announted that day. Ltn Wilhelm Frankl of *Jasta* 4 downed a fourth.

Bearing the white wheel hubs of a 'B' Flight aircraft from No 29 Sqn, this forlorn DH 2 attracts German attention after being brought down by Hptm Martin Zander of *Jasta* 1 on 25 August 1916. Its pilot, 2Lt K K Turner, was taken prisoner (*Greg VanWyngarden*)

Lts Robert H M S Saundby and Patrick A Langan-Byrne of No 24 Sqn. Although the aggressive Langan-Byrne was credited with ten victories, most were 'forced to land' – a category that the RFC would later cease to count (*Norman Franks*)

Ltn Otto Höhne sits in the cockpit of DH 2 7873 whilst Hptm Oswald Boelcke, commander of *Jasta* 2 (destined to be No 24 Sqn's bitterest rival) and Ltn Manfred *Freiherr* von Richthofen look on. Boelcke brought this aircraft down on 14 September 1916, its pilot, 2Lt J V Bowring of 'C' Flight, being wounded in action and duly taken prisoner (*Greg VanWyngarden*)

That night, a German army tradition was broken and a new air force tradition established when enlisted men were permitted to join the officers in the *Jasta* 2 *Kasino* to celebrate. Back at No 11 Sqn, Fred Libby lamented;

'This morning, Boelcke and his crew went into action on our "C" Flight. I knew it was too good to last, for the last few times we have been over, Price and I have had no action. Now with Mr Boelcke in his new and faster machines, we will really catch hell.'

Still, the Fees were not completely helpless. Shortly after he and Capt Price were awarded the MC 'for conspicuous gallantry while engaging and destroying enemy aircraft', Libby was serving as observer for Sgt Thompson on 22 September when they had a run-in with an Albatros over Bois de Longeast, which Libby drove down OOC. This might have been Ltn Eberhard Fügner of *Jasta* 4, who was severely wounded southeast of Bapaume.

One of No 24 Sqn's pilots was also becoming an ace at this time, as Lt Langan-Byrne, in DH 2 7911, was credited with an enemy aeroplane 'forced to land' on the 21st, two on the 22nd, one on the 23rd and another one on the 28th. These were encouraging moral victories, but the British would later cease

Born 9 February 1895, Stanley Cockerell came from Osterley Park, Middlesex, and joined No 24 Sqn as a sergeant in early 1916. He shared his first victory (a Fokker D II) with Lt A G Knight on 14 September, but was wounded on 10 October. Commissioned by the time he rejoined No 24 Sqn, he scored three more victories in DH 2s and one in a DH 5 before returning to England for Home Defence duty with Nos 50, 112 and 78 Sqns. Returning to France with No 151 Sqn (a Sopwith Camel-equipped night intruder unit), Capt Cockerell claimed his seventh victory on the night of 4 August 1918 when he ambushed a Gotha bomber that was coming in to land at Guizencourt aerodrome, which he had just bombed (*Norman Franks*)

counting them as they had little real impact on the enemy – as Langan-Byrne himself would soon find out.

——————— ACE DEBUTS IN 29 ———————

After several months of intermittent combat, No 29 Sqn acquired two new pilots of future distinction in the form of Lt G H Bowman and Flt Sgt J T B McCudden. On 3 September 'Beery' Bowman, as he was called due to his ruddy complexion, drove a Fokker E III away from the BE 2c that it was attacking east of Linselles and then found himself under attack by a Roland C II. Turning to meet it head-on, he apparently shot the pilot but the Roland careened on at him and struck his right wing, tearing away his aileron kingpost. In spite of the loss of lateral control, Bowman managed to nurse his DH 2 back home to be credited with his first victory.

On 6 September McCudden spotted a two-seater approaching the lines near Messines, and as it dived away east he gave chase. 'I got to within 400 yards', he wrote, 'but could not gain at all, although I could just hold him for speed, so I opened fire'. He ended up firing two more drums of ammunition before losing the still descending German in some clouds at 2000 ft above Gheluve. Three days after making out his report, however, an account from an Allied agent confirmed that a German aeroplane had crashed on the Menin road at Gheluve coincident with McCudden's recorded time and location.

He would not score again in 1916, but saw Bowman get his second on 27 September. A German observation balloon had broken loose and drifted toward Allied lines near Mount Kemmel. 2Lt Bowman and Sgt Jack Noakes were sent up after it. 'When Mr Bowman arrived he went baldheaded for the balloon and fairly filled it with incendiary bullets', McCudden wrote. 'The unfortunate Hun observer who was in the balloon, of course, went down with it in flames, but the height was not sufficient to kill him, and he was pulled away from the burning balloon by a lot of our Tommies, who had congregated to witness its demise.

'The climax occurred when Bowman went to land on the summit of Mount Kemmel to inspect his lawful prize and crashed completely,

DH 2s of No 29 Sqn are seen between patrols at Abeele aerodrome in August 1916. Flight colours applied to the wheels were supplemented in later September by individual numerals in those same colours on the nacelle sides and wings (*Greg VanWyngarden*)

Sgt James Thomas Byford McCudden (fourth from left) receives the *Croix de Guerre* for outstanding work as an observer with No 3 Sqn from Gen Joseph Joffre on 21 January 1916. Promoted to flight sergeant two days later, McCudden subsequently took pilot training and, after a short time with No 20 Sqn, joined 'C' Flight of No 29 Sqn. He scored five victories flying the DH 2 with this unit, and likely survived becoming von Richthofen's 15th victim on 27 December (*Norman Franks*)

The nacelle of DH 2 A2542 lies in German hands after being brought down on 16 October 1916 by Hptm Boelcke for his 34th victory. Its pilot, Lt P A Langan-Byrne, died of his wounds. The saw tooth design on the underside of the nacelle was a routinely seen on No 24 Sqn DH 2s (*Greg VanWyngarden*)

but fortunately without being hurt. He and his balloon were the subject of many jokes afterwards.'

Bowman claimed that upon landing he drew his revolver to take the German observer prisoner!

By the end of September 1916 the Albatros D II, combined with the adoption of Boelcke's tactical 'Dicta', had made *Jasta* 2 the vanguard of a general resurgence of German air power over the Western Front. Its ascendancy did not go undisputed, however – least of all by Hawker's No 24 Sqn.

In October Hawker placed Lt Langan-Byrne, who had been awarded the DSO, in command of 'B' Flight. At 1030 hrs on the 16th, Langan-Byrne forced an Albatros D I to land for his tenth official victory, but that afternoon *Jasta* 2 had a more fruitful day, with Boelcke and Offz Stv Leopold Reimann destroying BEs in the early afternoon and von Richthofen scoring his fifth – a BE 12 of No 19 Sqn – at 1700 hrs. Soon after that, Boelcke reported;

'We ran into six Vickers singleseaters south of Bapaume at 1745 hrs. We went into some fine turns. The English leader, with streamers on his machine, came right for me. I settled him with my first attack – apparently the pilot was killed, for the machine spun down.'

Boelcke's 34th victim was Langan-Byrne, the nacelle of whose DH 2, A2542, was later photographed intact, but who was killed and buried in a grave that has since gone unlocated. Sometime thereafter Maj Hawker sadly noted, 'I haven't recovered from the blow of losing him. He was such a nice lad, as well as the best officer I have ever met'.

No 11 Sqn was also having more encounters with *Jasta* 2. On 10 October 2Lt R P Harvey and Lt Libby were credited with an Albatros OOC, but *Jasta* 2 lost no men and Boelcke sent another No 11 Sqn crew down in flames. Capt Price and Lt Libby claimed another Albatros OOC on the 17th, but again the only documented losses were an FE 2b from No 23 Sqn and two from 11 Sqn, one of the latter being Boelcke's 35th victory. Price and Libby shared one more Albatros on the 20th, after which both men were posted back to England on well-deserved leave.

Capt Libby would return to the front as a pilot in 1917, scoring two victories in Sopwith 1½ Strutters whilst heading up No 43 Sqn's 'B' Flight, followed by two more in DH 4s leading 'B' Flight of No 25 Sqn, bringing his total to 14. He died in Los Angeles, California, on 9 January 1970, but not before writing a memoir in 1961 entitled *Horses Don't Fly* that was finally published in 2000.

On 26 October Hptm Boelcke's score reached 40. On the 28th, however, he met No 24 Sqn again, for what proved to be one time too many. Boelcke was leading a flight in response to a call for air support during an infantry attack when they encountered two 'C' Flight DH 2s, flown by Lt Alfred Gerald Knight, a 21-year-old English-born Canadian whose score then stood at six, and 2Lt Alfred Edwin McKay, credited with a Roland OOC on 20 July. In the swirling melee that followed, Boelcke and Böhme were converging on Knight when McKay, pursued by von Richthofen, flashed in front of them. As both Germans abruptly pulled up, Böhme's undercarriage struck Boelcke's left upper wing. Böhme regained control after falling 200 metres, but Boelcke's Albatros D II 386/16 went into an ever-steepening glide that ended in a fatal crash.

Oblt Stefan Kirmaier took over *Staffel* command. Although shaken by his loss, Boelcke's men would develop and expand upon his tactical principles, and take grim revenge on the RFC.

TWO MORE LEADERS FALL

At 1310 hrs on 22 November, 'Jock' Andrews shared his seventh victory with 2Lt Kelvin Crawford – an Albatros D II that the RFC communiqué described as 'a hostile machine, which crashed on our side of the lines near Les Boeufs'. Their victim, killed by a single bullet in the back of the head, turned out to be Oblt Stefan Kirmaier, who had scored his 11th victory just two days before, and who was last seen by his four accompanying pilots going after a 'Vikkers' two-seater.

Coming less than a month after Boelcke's death, Kirmaier's demise was a demoralising loss for *Jasta* 2. Special duty officer Oblt Karl Bodenschatz assumed administrative leadership until Oblt Franz Walz arrived as the new CO on the 29th, while Ltn Manfred von Richthofen, who had scored his ninth and tenth victories the same day as Kirmaier's last, became the *Kanone* to whom the *Staffel's* pilots now looked up to. It was a tacit but demanding role – but the next day von Richthofen fulfilled their expectations.

Capt Alfred Gerald Knight proved a fatal object of Hptm Oswald Boelcke's attention on 28 October 1916. Credited with eight victories, he had transferred to take command of 'B' Flight of No 29 Sqn when he became victim von Richthofen 13th victim on 20 December (*Norman Franks*)

After service in the Durham Light Infantry, Seldon Herbert Long joined No 29 Sqn, with whom he downed a Fokker Eindecker on 6 August 1916. Late that year Capt Long transferred to No 24 Sqn, and added another eight to his tally between 16 November 1916 and 6 March 1917. After returning home, 'Tubby' Long flew Sopwith Pups with No 46 Sqn, commanded No 111 Sqn in Palestine and wrote a book (*In The Blue*) about his experiences in 1920, before leaving the RAF as a major (*Norman Franks*)

Twelve-victory ace Capt John Oliver Andrews of No 24 Sqn poses with his DH 2 at Bertangles in late 1916 (*Aaron Weaver*)

Pilots of *Jasta* 2 are seen with Ltn Manfred von Richthofen's Albatros D II 391/16. They are, from left to right, Oblt Stefan Kirmaier (Boelcke's successor as *Staffelführer*), Ltn Hans Imelmann, von Richthofen and Ltn Hans Wortmann. On 22 November Kirmaier fell victim to DH 2s of No 24 Sqn, but von Richthofen took a more precise revenge than he initially realised the following day when he killed the unit's famous CO, Maj Lanoe Hawker (*Greg VanWyngarden*)

At 1300 hrs on the 23rd, Andrews led four 'A' Flight DH 2s, flown by Capt Saundby, 2Lt John H Crutch and, as a last-minute replacement, the squadron CO, Maj Hawker (in 5964), off on a patrol from Bertangles. At 1330 hrs Crutch's engine began knocking, and he made a precautionary landing at No 9 Sqn's field near Morlancourt, where he found 'plugs damaged and tappet rods out of adjustment' in two cylinders.

Continuing on, 'A' Flight encountered two 'HA' (hostile aircraft) northeast of Bapaume at 1350 hrs and drove them east until Andrews looked up and noticed 'two strong patrols of HA scouts above me'. He judged it prudent to disengage, but reported 'A DH Scout, flown by Maj Hawker, dived past me and continued to pursue'. Figuring Hawker had not noticed the enemy fighters, and loath to abandon their commander, Andrews and Saundby followed him and, as Andrews noted, 'were at once attacked by the HA, one of which dived onto Maj Hawker's tail'.

In what he described as a 'violent fight', Saundby was jumped by two Albatros D IIs, which forced him to spiral 'two or three times'. Andrews drove off Hawker's assailant after firing 25 rounds at close range, but was himself attacked by a fourth Albatros that crippled his engine. As he tried to glide away, 'obliged to try to regain our lines', Andrews' DH was further shot about until Saundby came to the rescue, firing a double drum of Lewis rounds into the pursuing Albatros at 20 yards' range until it 'wobbled' and then power-dived away. Although *Jasta* 2 recorded no corresponding casualty, the Albatros was credited to Saundby as 'OOC' for his third victory.

Before crossing the lines to made a dead-stick landing at Guillemont at 1410 hrs, Andrews claimed to have last seen his CO 'at about 3000 ft near Bapaume, fighting with an HA, apparently quite under control but going down'. The only other witness to Hawker's last fight was Manfred von Richthofen;

'I attacked, together with two other aeroplanes, a Vickers one-seater at 3000 metres altitude. After a long curve fight of three to five minutes, I had forced down my adversary to 500 metres. He now tried to escape, flying to the Front. I pursued and brought him down after 900 shots.'

That terse combat report was considerably elaborated upon after von Richthofen learned the identity of his 11th victim. 'The gallant fellow was full of pluck', he wrote, 'and when we had got down to about 3000 ft he

DH 2 5925 'blue 4' of No 29 Sqn was brought down intact northeast of Wancourt on 9 November as the ninth, and last, victory for Ltn Gustav Leffers of *Jasta* 1. Its pilot, 2Lt Ivan Curlewis, had burned a balloon on 1 October prior to becoming a PoW. On 27 December Leffers' luck ran out when he took on an FE 2b crewed by Capt John Bowley Quested and 2Lt H J H Dicksee of No 11 Sqn (*Greg VanWyngarden*)

merrily waved at me as if he was saying "Well – how do you do"?' Seemingly stalemated between the DH 2's agility versus the Albatros' brisker speed and climb, both adversaries knew that the prevailing westerly winds and the possibility of more Germans intervening compelled the British pilot to choose between force landing in enemy territory or making a break for home. 'Of course he tried the latter', von Richthofen wrote, but as Hawker zig-zagged away at a height of 300 ft, the German ace added, 'the jamming of my gun nearly robbed me of my success'. The 900 rounds he fired confirm the Baron's claim that this had indeed been his most difficult combat to date.

German Grenadiers found and buried the man von Richthofen justly called the 'English Boelcke' 250 yards east of the Luisenhof Farm on the Flers road. Like Kirmaier the day before, he had died from a single bullet in the back of the head.

By December 1916 No 29 Sqn was having its own share of encounters with *Jasta* 2, which in that month was renamed *Jasta* 'Boelcke' or *Jasta* 'B' in honour of its late 'founding father'. Indeed, one of squadron's aces and very likely a future ace in its ranks had run-ins with the German unit's rising star, Manfred von Richthofen.

Soon after scoring his seventh victory on 6 November, Lt 'Jerry' Knight of No 24 Sqn was promoted to captain and made a flight commander in No 29 Sqn. On 16 December he attacked two enemy aeroplanes and downed one and was game enough to take on the other when his machine gun extractor fractured, forcing him to disengage.

Knight was slated for ten days' leave after completing a patrol on 20 December, but he did not return. All four of the DH 2s he had led off on patrol came back to Le Hameau aerodrome badly shot up, 2Lt H B Hurst having to make an emergency landing in A2552 south of Beaumetz. Knight's fate was reported by his killer, Ltn Richthofen of *Jasta* 'Boelcke';

'About 1130 hrs I attacked, together with four aeroplanes, at 3000 metres altitude an enemy one-seater above Monchy-au-Bois. After some curve fighting I managed to press my adversary down to 1500 metres, where I attacked him at closest range (aeroplane length). I saw immediately

This No 32 Sqn DH 2 (7862) is seen here equipped with what appear to be Le Prieur rockets, although they seem to be lacking their warheads. These weapons were usually employed against observation balloons (*Aaron Weaver*)

that I had hit the enemy. First he went down in curves, then he crashed to the ground. I pursued him until 100 metres above the ground.'

One week later, on 27 December, Capt Harold J Payn was leading six DH 2s of 'C' Flight on a patrol from Arras to Monchy, where the Canadian Corps was engaging in a major raid, when it got into a fight with some Albatros D IIs and Flt Sgt McCudden went to the aid of Lt Alexander Jennings, who had a D II on his tail.

'I now fired at the nearest Hun who was after Jennings', McCudden wrote, 'and this Hun at once came for me nose-on, and we both fired simultaneously, but after firing about 20 shots my gun got a bad double feed, which I could not recify at the time as I was now in the middle of five D I Albatroses, so I half-rolled.

'When coming out I kept the machine past vertical for a few hundred feet and had started to level out again when "cack, cack, cack" came from just behind me, and on looking round I saw my old friend with the black and white streamers again. I immediately half-rolled again, but still the Hun stayed there, and so whilst half-rolling I kept on making headway for our lines, for the fight had started east of Adinfer Wood, with which we were so familiar on our previous little joy-jaunts. I continued to do half-rolls and got over the trenches at about 2000 ft, with the Hun still in pursuit, and the rascal drove me down to 800 ft a mile west of the lines, at which point he turned off east and was shelled by our AA guns. I soon rectified the jamb and turned to chase the Hun, crossing the trenches at 2000 ft, but by this time the Hun was much higher, and very soon joined his patrol, who were waiting for him at 5000 ft over Ransart.

'Soon after landing I met Capt (G T R) Hill, who looked at me as at a ghost. "What?" he said. "You, here? Why, Payn has just said that you went down out of control over Hunland, with a big fat Hun in attendance". "Yes", I replied, "so I did – that is why I am here"!'

McCudden's dive, which seems to have looked as terminal to his comrades as it must have to enemy witnesses, suggests that his DH 2 was the 'Vickers two-seater' credited to von Richthofen at that time and place. 'At 1615 hrs', the Baron reported, 'five aeroplanes of our *Staffel* attacked an enemy squadron south of Arras. The enemy approached our lines, but was thrown back. After some fighting I managed to attack a very courageously flown Vickers two-seater. After 300 shots, the enemy aeroplane began dropping, uncontrolled. I pursued it up to 1000 metres above the ground. The aeroplane crashed to the ground on the enemy side of the line, one kilometre behind the trenches near Ficheux'.

Hours before McCudden had survived becoming von Richthofen's 15th victim, the Germans had suffered a more permanent loss to a pusher. Capt John Bowley Quested and 2Lt H J H Dicksee of No 11 Sqn were returning from a reconnaissance mission when they were attacked by fighters of *Jasta* 1. During the melee Dicksee downed what he identified as a Nieuport near Wancourt, which turned out to indeed be a captured Nieuport 16 flown by nine-victory ace, and *Pour le Mérite* recipient, Ltn Gustav Leffers, who was killed. At 1230 hrs Vzfw Wilhelm Cymera forced Quested and Dicksee's FE 2b 7666 down in British lines, but like McCudden they lived to tell the tale – and, for that matter, to down another enemy fighter OOC on 25 January 1917 for Quested's eighth victory.

Born in Cheriton, Kent, on 14 December 1893, John Bowley Quested was credited with eight victories flying FE 2bs with No 11 Sqn. One of his victims was German ace Gustav Leffers. Injured whilst serving with No 40 Sqn, and again while commanding No 1 Aerial Gunnery Range in France, Maj Quested served briefly with No 48 Sqn in Quetta, India, in 1919, before retiring to take up farming in East Anglia. He died on 11 March 1948 (*Norman Franks*)

Jimmy McCudden went on to get an officer's commission in January 1917. 'Those shows I liked, so long as I came out of them', he remarked, 'but it was no fun fighting an enemy who was 15 mph faster and had almost twice the rate of climb'. Nevertheless, he managed to score four more victories in the obsolescent DH 2s between 26 January and 15 February 1917, subsequently coming into his full stride in SE 5as with No 56 Sqn. McCudden had raised his score to 57, and received the VC, by the time he lost his life in a crash at Auxi-le-Château on 10 July 1918.

AVENGING HAWKER

The DH 2 was patently obsolete as 1917 dawned, yet Nos 24, 29 and 32 Sqns were forced to get by with their pushers well into the year, including throughout 'Bloody April'. In spite of that, in the first months of 1917 No 24 Sqn's pilots scored some remarkable successes against their long-time nemeses at *Jasta* 'Boelcke'.

A DH 2 of No 29 Sqn is serviced at Le Hameau in early 1917 (*P Jarrett*)

Ex-No 24 Sqn DH 2 5925 sits disarmed for training duties at Brooklands, the fighter still displaying remnants of its 'A' Flight wheel and interplane strut markings. Assigned to No 24 Sqn from February 1916 through to May 1917, this remarkable veteran scored victories with a number of aces, including Lt P A Langan-Byrne on 16 October, 2Lt Eric C Pashley on 3 November, 2Lt Kelvin Crawford on 22 November 1916 and 2 April 1917 and Lt Robert H M S Saundby on 23 November (*Greg VanWyngarden*)

This photo of DH 2 7851 of No 32 Sqn was taken shortly after it had been brought down on 7 January 1917 by Ltn Erwin Böhme of *Jasta* 'Boelcke'. Its pilot, 2Lt F G Wagner, apparently died from the wounds he suffered in this action. The black wheel hub with a white disc in the centre denotes the fighter's assignment to 'C' Flight. This was also signified by a white letter 'C' painted onto the underside of the nacelle (*Colin Owers*)

An original member of No 32 Sqn, 2Lt William George Sellar Curphey downed German two-seaters on 22 August and 28 and 30 September 1916. Promoted to captain in early 1917, he downed two Albatros D IIs during a fight with *Jasta* 'Boelcke' on 4 February, one of his victims probably being Ltn Christian von Scheele. Curphey was in turn downed by Ltn Erwin Böhme with a slight head wound. Quickly recovering from this minor setback, he shared in the destruction of another D II with Lt H D Davis on 7 February. During a dogfight with six Albatros D IIs on 14 May, a squadronmate drove an attacker off Curphey's tail, but he was promptly jumped by another, flown by *Jasta* 'Boelcke' commander Hptm Franz Walz. The latter pilot shot him down in flames east of Lagnicourt for his seventh victory (*Norman Franks*)

On 23 January, Lt Eric Clowes Pashley from London, who had scored five victories between 3 November and 11 December 1916, shot down an Albatros D III that was attacking a BE near Grandcourt. Its pilot, Vfw Paul Ostrop of *Jasta* 'B', died of his wounds. The next day, Capt H A Wood and Lt Alfred McKay brought down a two-seater near Thiepval whose pilot, Uffz Max August Delklock, held off approaching British troops with his pistol until his observer Ltn Ernst Bury, had time to burn their aeroplane, after which they surrendered.

Flugmt Gustav Kinkel, a naval pilot attached to *Jasta* 'B', had just scored his first victory over an FE 2d on 25 January when a DH 2 drove him down south of Bapaume, where he too was captured and his Albatros D III 1982/16 seized intact – he was McKay's fourth victory. That same day Capt Selden Long downed an LVG from *Fl Abt (A)* 216 in flames between Bapaume and Clery, its crewmen, Ltns d R Ernst Erdmann and Günter Kallenbach, jumping to their deaths. Long destroyed another two-seater near Bapaume 48 hours later, killing Vzfw Willy Lang and Ltn Kurt Brandt of *Fl Abt (A)* 233.

Jasta 'B' scored four victories on 4 February, but its day was spoilt by the death of Ltn Christian von Scheele, who was attacking FE 2bs of No 22 Sqn when he was killed near Le Mesnil. He was the seventh victory for No 24 Sqn's Lt Eric Pashley, who shared his demise with one of the FE crews.

No 32 Sqn also had some run-ins with *Jasta* 'B' on the 4th, Capt William G S Curphey claiming two Albatros – one shared with Capt James M Robb and Lt H D Davis – before being shot about and returning to his aerodrome at Léalvillers with a head wound, possibly caused by Ltn Böhme. Capt Hubert W G Jones claimed an Albatros OOC over Grevillers the next day, which might have been *Jasta* 'B's' Vzfw Thiel, who was lightly wounded.

1

Voisin 3LA V89 of Sgt Joseph Frantz
and *Soldat* Louis Quénault, V24, Lery,
October 1914

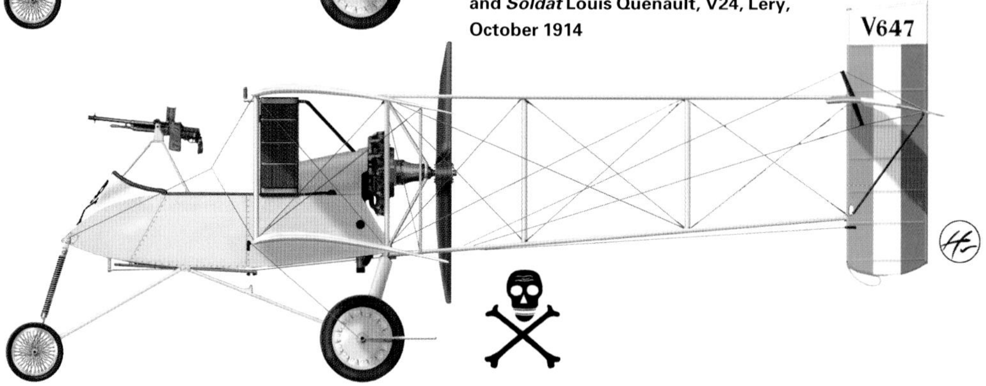

2

Voisin 3LAS V647 of Adj Charles Nungesser and
Soldat Roger Pochon, VB106, Dunkerque, July 1915

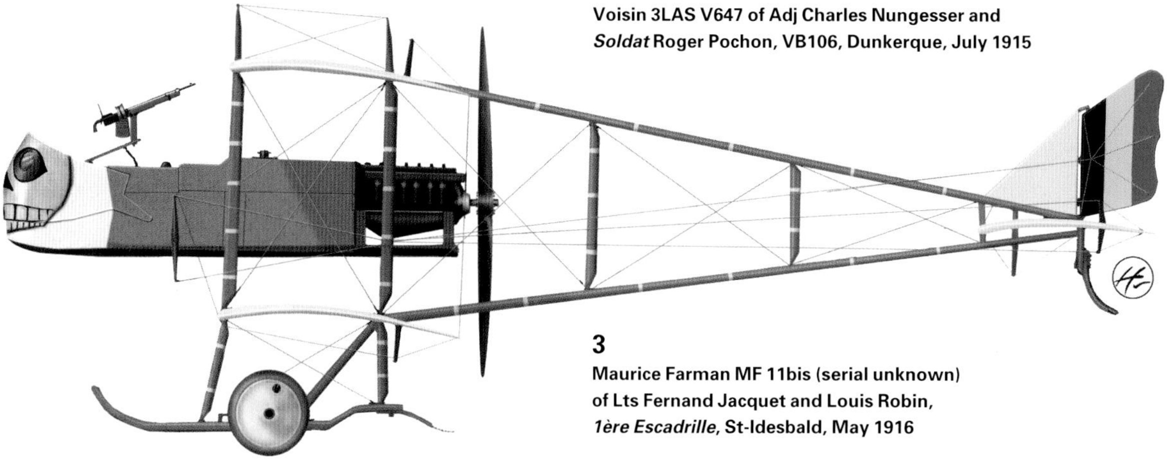

3

Maurice Farman MF 11bis (serial unknown)
of Lts Fernand Jacquet and Louis Robin,
1ère Escadrille, St-Idesbald, May 1916

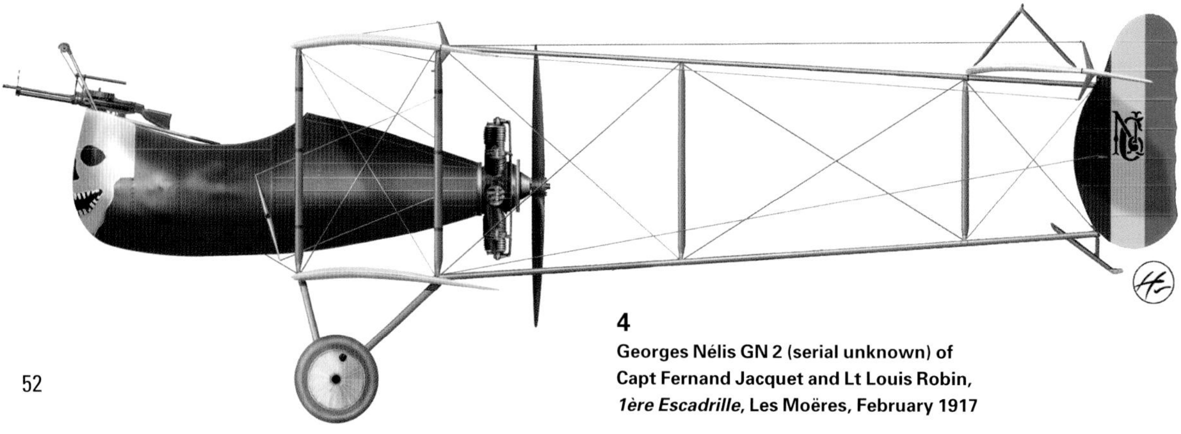

4

Georges Nélis GN 2 (serial unknown) of
Capt Fernand Jacquet and Lt Louis Robin,
1ère Escadrille, Les Moëres, February 1917

52

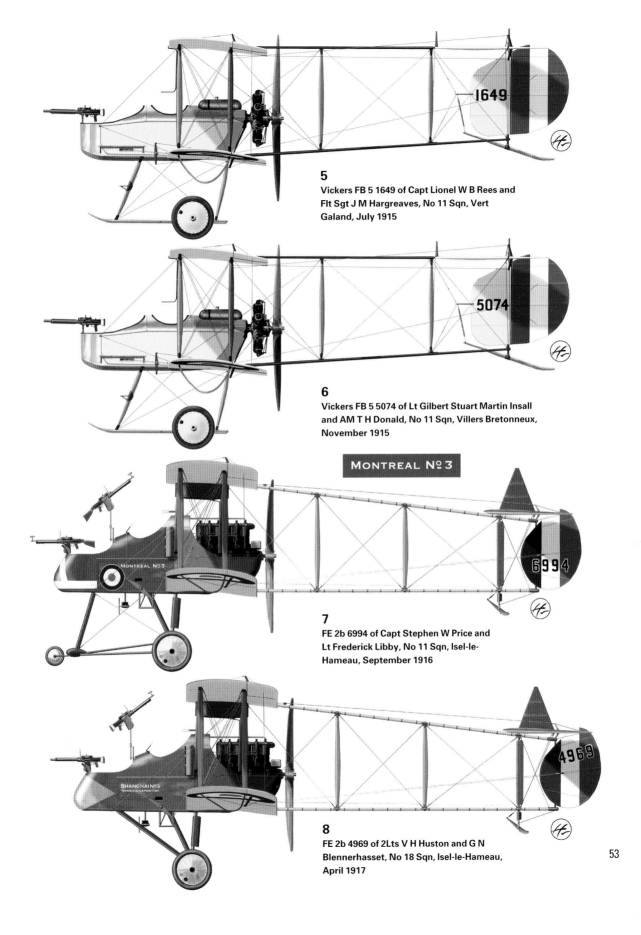

5
Vickers FB 5 1649 of Capt Lionel W B Rees and
Flt Sgt J M Hargreaves, No 11 Sqn, Vert
Galand, July 1915

6
Vickers FB 5 5074 of Lt Gilbert Stuart Martin Insall
and AM T H Donald, No 11 Sqn, Villers Bretonneux,
November 1915

7
FE 2b 6994 of Capt Stephen W Price and
Lt Frederick Libby, No 11 Sqn, Isel-le-
Hameau, September 1916

8
FE 2b 4969 of 2Lts V H Huston and G N
Blennerhasset, No 18 Sqn, Isel-le-Hameau,
April 1917

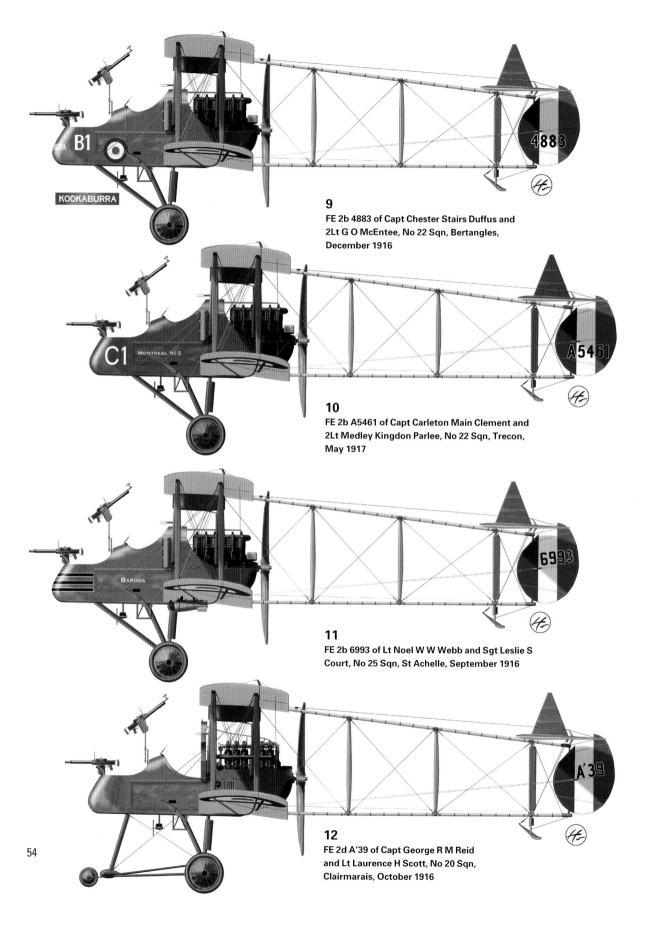

9
FE 2b 4883 of Capt Chester Stairs Duffus and
2Lt G O McEntee, No 22 Sqn, Bertangles,
December 1916

10
FE 2b A5461 of Capt Carleton Main Clement and
2Lt Medley Kingdon Parlee, No 22 Sqn, Trecon,
May 1917

11
FE 2b 6993 of Lt Noel W W Webb and Sgt Leslie S
Court, No 25 Sqn, St Achelle, September 1916

12
FE 2d A'39 of Capt George R M Reid
and Lt Laurence H Scott, No 20 Sqn,
Clairmarais, October 1916

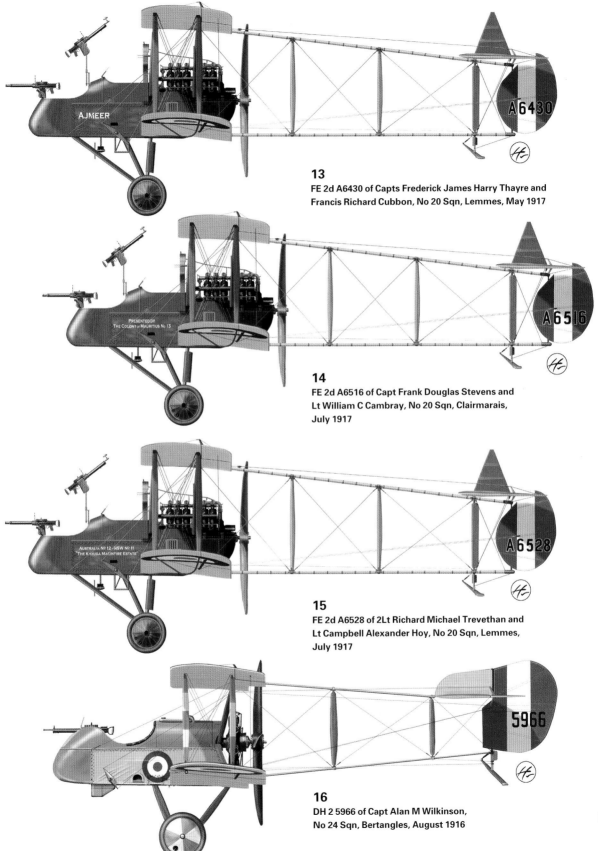

13
FE 2d A6430 of Capts Frederick James Harry Thayre and
Francis Richard Cubbon, No 20 Sqn, Lemmes, May 1917

14
FE 2d A6516 of Capt Frank Douglas Stevens and
Lt William C Cambray, No 20 Sqn, Clairmarais,
July 1917

15
FE 2d A6528 of 2Lt Richard Michael Trevethan and
Lt Campbell Alexander Hoy, No 20 Sqn, Lemmes,
July 1917

16
DH 2 5966 of Capt Alan M Wilkinson,
No 24 Sqn, Bertangles, August 1916

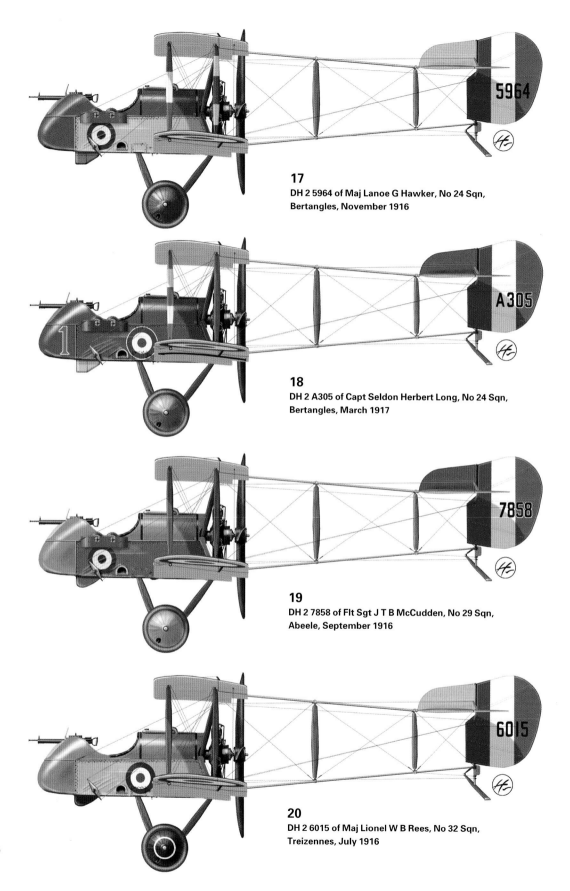

17
DH 2 5964 of Maj Lanoe G Hawker, No 24 Sqn,
Bertangles, November 1916

18
DH 2 A305 of Capt Seldon Herbert Long, No 24 Sqn,
Bertangles, March 1917

19
DH 2 7858 of Flt Sgt J T B McCudden, No 29 Sqn,
Abeele, September 1916

20
DH 2 6015 of Maj Lionel W B Rees, No 32 Sqn,
Treizennes, July 1916

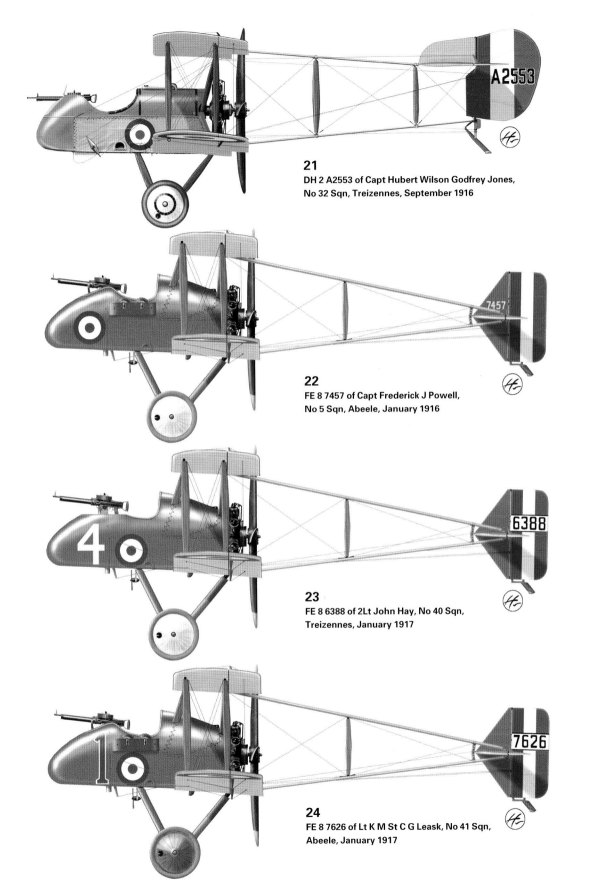

21
DH 2 A2553 of Capt Hubert Wilson Godfrey Jones,
No 32 Sqn, Treizennes, September 1916

22
FE 8 7457 of Capt Frederick J Powell,
No 5 Sqn, Abeele, January 1916

23
FE 8 6388 of 2Lt John Hay, No 40 Sqn,
Treizennes, January 1917

24
FE 8 7626 of Lt K M St C G Leask, No 41 Sqn,
Abeele, January 1917

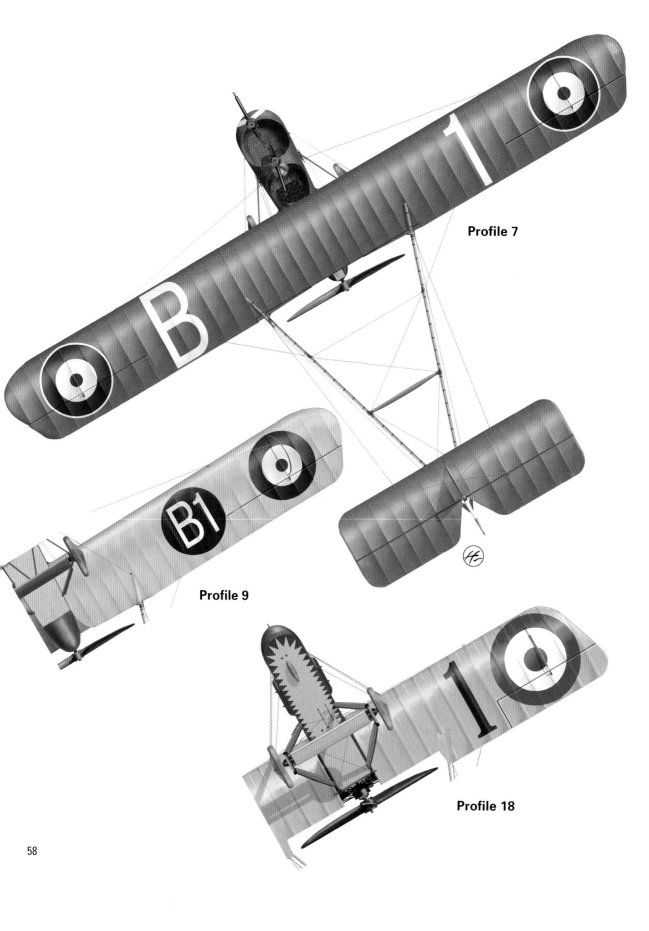

Profile 7

Profile 9

Profile 18

58

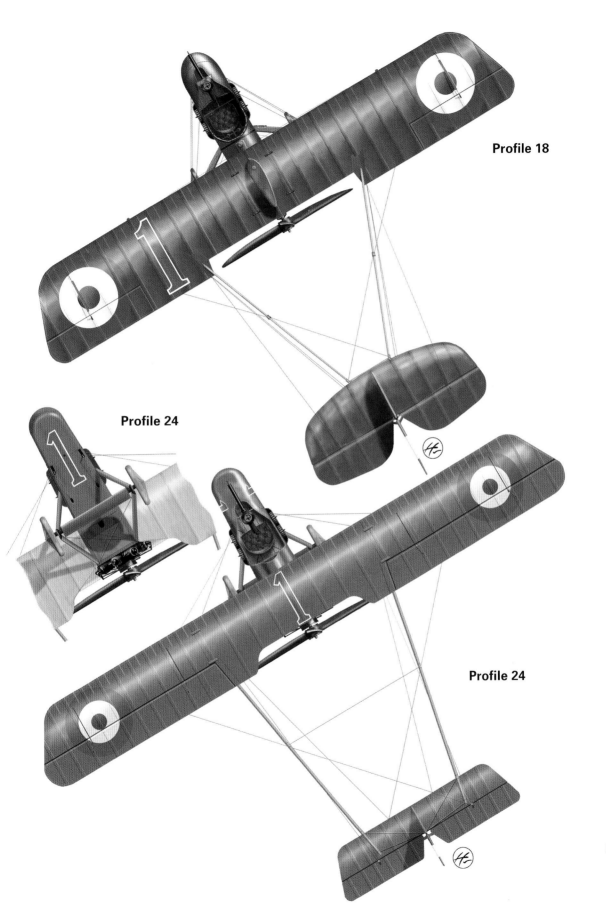

Profile 18

Profile 24

Profile 24

59

PUSHERS IN DECLINE

T he Battle of the Somme was probably the pusher fighters' moment of glory as they wrested control of the sky from the Fokker Eindeckers – but it was short-lived glory all the same. During the autumn of 1916 the Albatros D II established the single-seat tractor engine biplane as the most efficient killing machine in the sky, and although some DH 2 pilots added substantially to their scores in the first few months of 1917, by 'Bloody April' it was painfully clear that the pusher scout had outlived its usefulness.

The same could certainly be said for the two-seat FE 2b and FE 2d as well, yet the first half of 1917 saw them score some of their most spectacular successes before experiencing a change of mission that saw them used as night intruders.

While the FE 2b and FE 2d had been muddling through on the Western Front, the Royal Aircraft Factory had been working on a single-seat variation that in some respects was better than Airco's DH 2. However, by the time the FE 8 reached the front in squadron strength, the pusher fighter in general had been eclipsed, and even the best of the pilots flying the new machine would find themselves 'up against it'.

First flown on 15 October 1915, the FE 8 had wings whose dihedral began outboard of the inner set of interplane struts and whose four-foot chord gave them a relatively high aspect ratio. Aluminium was used for the nacelle, the bottom of which was armoured, and steel tubing was used for the tail booms, struts and tail framing. Power, as with the DH 2, came from a 100 hp Gnome monosoupape rotary engine.

This is FE 8 6454, which was assigned to No 41 Sqn on 13 November 1916. After arriving at Abeele aerodrome on 21 October 1916, No 41 Sqn suffered its first loss on 26 November when 2Lt George S Deane's engine misfired, he became lost in cloud while trying to get back and he force landed near Roulers when he ran low on fuel. In spite of Deane's attempts to burn the fighter prior to fleeing the scene, the FE 8 was recovered completely intact by German infantry. Deane was also captured (*Aaron Weaver*)

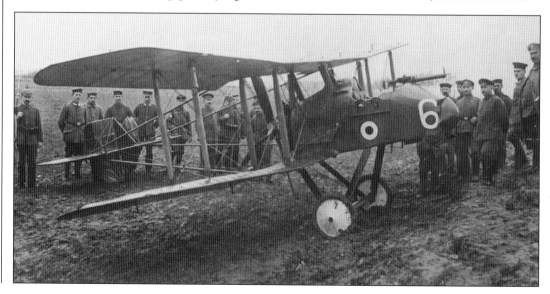

Shown in the centre of this photograph whilst serving as a flight leader with No 40 Sqn, Capt Frederick James Powell had previously been credited with two victories in FB 5s and four while evaluation flying FE 8 7457 with No 5 Sqn. Later commanding No 41 Sqn, Powell was brought down by *Jasta* 10's Ltn Max Kühn on 2 February 1918 and captured (*Aaron Weaver*)

The first two FE 8 prototypes mounted Lewis guns within their nacelles, but following their frontline evaluation with No 5 Sqn that arrangement reverted to a mount above the front of the nacelle as per the DH 2. The second prototype – 7457 – had a spinner fitted to its four-bladed propeller when it was sent to No 5 Sqn at Abeele on 26 December 1915, but this had been removed by mid-January.

Throughout its frontline evaluation 7457 was flown almost exclusively by Capt Frederick James Powell. He had previously piloted FB 5s with the squadron and claimed an Ago destroyed on 19 September 1915, as well as three enemy aeroplanes 'driven down' and four others 'driven off,' from which reports two victories were officially confirmed and Powell awarded the MC. He used the new FE 8 quite aggressively and rather possessively, allegedly declining an opportunity to go on leave rather than risk another pilot flying 'his' aeroplane!

A French soldier examines an FE 8 of 'C' Flight, No 40 Sqn. Although superior to the DH 2 in some respects, the FE 8 was seriously outclassed by the time it reached the Western Front in quantity (*Jon Guttman*)

Powell used 7457 to send down an Aviatik OOC near Becelaere on 17 January 1916. Less than three weeks later, on 5 February, he drove down an Aviatik, chased an Albatros back over German lines and forced down an LVG. The latter was confirmed as a victory, although an Albatros 'driven down' two days later was not. Powell 'made ace' on 29 February, when he destroyed an Aviatik in flames near Passchendaele, and a Fokker Eindecker 'driven down' on 12 March was credited as his sixth victory.

Ironically, although Powell was later made a flight commander in No 40 Sqn and CO of No 41 Sqn on 2 August 1917, he added no more victories to his score prior to being brought down wounded at Auber-chicourt in SE 5a B8273 on 2 February 1918 by Ltn Max Kühn of *Jasta* 10. Following nine months in a PoW camp, Powell served postwar with No 28 Sqn in India. Becoming an Officer of the Order of the British Empire in later life, he lived in Dorset until he passed away in May 1992, aged 96.

SOLE FE 8 ACE

At least six FE 8s were allotted to No 29 Sqn, but none of them lasted long, mostly due to crashes. One of the first to be lost was 6378, which was shot down on 22 June 1916 and its pilot, Capt L H Sweet, killed. Built by the Royal Aircraft Factory, Darracq and Vickers, production FE 8s were issued to two units organised at Gosport specifically to use them – No 40 Sqn, formed in February 1916, and No 41 Sqn, created five months later.

On 25 August No 40 Sqn arrived at Treizennes aerodrome. Its commander, pre-war actor Maj Robert Lorraine, strongly believed in carrying the fight to the enemy, so he had his pilots trained to perform night landings and encouraged them to experiment with the improve-ment of the armament fitted to their aircraft. The unit enjoyed its first success on 22 September when Capt D O Mulholland, in FE 8 6384, came to the aid of an FE 2b of No 25 Sqn and shot down a 'Fokker E III'

FE 8 7624 was much photographed after falling into German hands on 9 November 1916. Its pilot, 22-year-old Capt Thomas George Mapplebeck, came from Liverpool and served with the 49th The Kings Regiment until 15 April 1915, when, he said, 'At Ypres I was hit in the mouth by a German dentist with a Mauser and lost most of my teeth'. Taking up flight training at Farnborough after reasoning that 'If I can drive a car I can drive an aeroplane', he claimed two victories in DH 2s with No 29 Sqn, before transferring to No 40 Sqn in September 1916. On 9 November he said, 'I crossed the lines at 200 ft, put a drum of Lewis ammunition into the bottom of a balloon, changed the drum, attacked, and the observer parachuted as I sent the balloon down in flames'. Ltn Erwin Böhme was subsequently credited with having downed 7624 for his sixth victory, but Mapplebeck claimed, 'I took a rifle bullet in my petrol pressure pipe and was forced to land and be taken prisoner'. Mapplebeck spent the rest of the war in Osnabück, Schweinitz ('where I spent five-and-a-half-months in solitary for constantly organising escapes') and Silesia. During World War 2 he was RAF liaison officer in Yugoslavia (*Aaron Weaver*)

near Douai. The German pilot involved, Oblt Karl Albert of *KEK 3*, was actually flying an E IV when he was shot down and killed. His demise was also credited to the crew of FE 2b 6998, Cpl Thomas Mottershead and 2Lt C Street.

Another pilot who took Lorraine's aggressive tactical philosophy to heart was Lt Edwin Louis Benbow. Born in December 1895 and raised in London, he had previously served for a year with the Royal Field Artillery from February 1915, before transferring to the RFC and spending eight months as an observer. Benbow eventually got the chance to train as a pilot, and he was assigned to No 40 Sqn. His first success came on 20 October 1916 when he destroyed an Albatros D II east of Lens. He downed a two-seater in flames near Vimy two days later, followed by an Albatros two-seater destroyed between Provin and Annoeullin on 16 November, the latter possibly leaving Gfr Josef Eiberger and Ltn Jäger of *Fl Abt (A)* 250 wounded.

On 4 December Mulholland and Benbow were each credited with a D II destroyed northeast of Arras, one of which may have been flown by Vfw Wilhelm Hennebeil of *Jasta* 12, who was killed. Another victory over a two-seater Albatros on 20 December made 'Lobo' Benbow the first, and only, pilot to 'make ace' on the FE 8 – all in 7627.

It should be noted at this point that while the FE 8 was as capable as the DH 2 when Fred Powell had flown it in January 1916, the 'state of the art' in terms of fighter technology had advanced apace by January 1917, and it would take an outstanding breed of pusher pilot to carry on thereafter. One such man was Australian 2Lt John Hay, who was born on 22 January 1889 in the Sydney suburb of Double Bay. After gaining his pilot's certificate on 2 June 1916 and being posted to No 40 Sqn, 'Jack' Hay proved a brave and resourceful aviator, scoring his third victory (an Albatros two-seater) at 1015 hrs on 23 January 1917. At 1312 hrs that afternoon, he joined another patrol that had been charged with escorting a photographic aeroplane over the Lens area. It would prove to be a fatal rendezvous.

At 1345 hrs Benbow engaged a two-seater south of La Bassée and drove it east. Sometime around 1500 hrs, he saw eight enemy aeroplanes 2000 ft below him as he patrolled west of Lens. He and another FE 8 dived to attack, but Benbow's gun jammed and as he turned to rectify it, he found himself attacked head-on by a red machine. Benbow dived to evade, got his Lewis working and turned to rejoin the fight, only to see the enemy retiring eastward.

Meanwhile, at 1505 hrs GMT, Hay's FE 8 6388 had fallen in flames two miles east of Aix Noulette, where his remains were recovered by Canadian troops. He was Ltn Manfred von Richthofen's first victim since the latter's transfer to take command of *Jasta* 11 at Brayelles three days earlier. It was also the *Staffel's* first victory.

'At about 1610 hrs I attacked, together with seven of my aeroplanes, enemy squadrons, west of Lens', von Richthofen reported. 'The aero plane I had singled out caught fire after 150 shots, fired from a distance of 50 metres. It fell, burning. The occupant fell out of the aeroplane at a height of 500 metres.'

Hay was also the first victim of von Richthofen's Albatros D III 789/16, which he had just recently received and had overpainted in red.

One of No 40 Sqn's more successful FE 8 pilots was 2Lt John Hay, shown here in 6388. He scored his third victory on the morning of 23 January 1917 in this machine, and was also flying it when he was killed that same afternoon by the newly appointed *Staffelführer* of *Jasta* 11, Ltn Manfred von Richthofen (*Jon Guttman*)

Inspired by the manoeuvrability and improved downward vision of the Nieuport 17, the Albatros design team had tried to achieve the best of both worlds by applying a similar sesquiplane wing arrangement to the D II. The resulting D III did show an improvement in both appearance and performance, but at a price that von Richthofen himself almost paid on 24 January, when he brought down an FE 2b of No 25 Sqn west of Vimy. The wounded crew of Capt Oscar Greig and Lt John E Maclennan were taken prisoner.

Von Richthofen landed nearby, but not to chat with his victims or take a souvenir. During the fight his lower wing had failed as a result of a disturbing tendency that saw it twist about on its axis during a prolonged dive. While Albatros hastily took steps to reinforce the D III's lower wing, von Richthofen mostly flew a Halberstadt D II until the very end of March 1917.

Switching to FE 8 A4871, 'Lobo' Benbow resumed his scoring on 14 February, when he and Canadian-born Lt G C O Usborne downed an Albatros D II east of Arras. Benbow drove another D II down OOC west of Douai the following day.

On 4 March Lt Saundby, who had been transferred to No 41 Sqn from No 24 Sqn on 26 January 1917, was flying in FE 8 6431 when he and 2Lt Andrew Fraser, in 7622, saw a Nieuport being attacked by an Albatros, which dived down past Saundby's nose. The latter dived on the German's tail and fired 25 rounds as the range increased from 40 to 100 yards. Fraser, who was lower, emptied a drum into the Albatros, which they saw crash east of Polygon Wood. German records do not identify that victim, but that same day Ltn Max Böhme of *Jasta* 5 became a PoW after his Albatros D II 910/16 was brought down intact by the combined efforts of DH 2 pilot 2Lt Arthur J Pearson of No 29 Sqn and the FE 2b crew of Lts Braham and James A V Boddy of No 11 Sqn.

On 6 March *Jasta* 11 Halberstadts attacked a flight of Sopwith 1$^1/_2$ Strutters of No 43 Sqn, Ltn d R Karl Emil Schäfer sending one down in flames and getting credit for a second that crashed in Allied lines. Von Richthofen was closing on another Sopwith when he heard an abrupt bang, followed by the odour of petrol that was now squirting around his legs and feet. Diving

away trailing petrol vapour, he landed at Henin-Liétard, where he found his engine to be damaged and both fuel tanks riddled and drained. On the way down von Richthofen noticed another Halberstadt spinning away, whose pilot, Ltn Eduard Lübbert, had suffered a shoulder wound and a glancing blow to the chest, but had still managed to land safely.

Von Richthofen's and Lübbert's assailants had been FE 8s of No 40 Sqn, Lt Benbow being credited with a 'flamer' and Capt Robert Gregory a Halberstadt that dived away vertically. Lübbert was apparently also credited to the Sopwith crew of Lt Harold H Balfour and 2Lt A Roberts. It seems somehow apt that Benbow's eighth, and last, victory was over the man who had killed his squadronmate Jack Hay almost two months earlier – and somewhat of a blow to the 'Red Baron's' aura of invincibility for the bargain – but things would go differently for No 40 Sqn's FEs three days later.

By 9 March No 40 Sqn had claimed 16 enemy aeroplanes destroyed and seven OOC. At 0845 hrs that morning, ten FE 8s took off from Treizennes, although 2Lt Leonard P Blaxland subsequently had to head home when a rocker arm in his engine broke. The remaining nine FEs encountered eight Albatros D IIs of *Jasta* 11, led by von Richthofen.

On 6 March 1917, Capt Robert Gregory of No 40 Sqn claimed a Halberstadt, as did the crew (Lt Harold H Balfour and 2Lt A Roberts) of the No 45 Sqn Sopwith 1¹/₂ Strutter that it was attacking. Their victim was apparently Ltn Eduard Lübbert of *Jasta* 11, who suffered a shoulder wound and a glancing blow to the chest, but managed to land safely. In the same action, Lt 'Lobo' Benbow claimed his eighth victory, which may have been Lübbert's *Staffelführer*, Manfred von Richthofen (*Norman Franks*)

Part of *Jasta* 11's revenge for its embarrassing setback of 6 March 1917, FE 8 A4874 'Blue 4' of No 40 Sqn undergoes German scrutiny after being brought down by Ltn Karl Emil Schäfer on 9 March. Its pilot, 2Lt G F Heseler, was taken prisoner (*Greg VanWyngarden*)

Another No 40 Sqn victim of *Jasta* 11's 9 March rampage was FE 8 6456 'Red 4', flown by 2Lt T Shepard, which was brought down by Ltn Kurt Wolff. Like his squadronmate 2 Lt Heseler, Shepard also became a PoW (*Greg VanWyngarden*)

Lt Meredith Thomas flew FE 8 4925 'White 2' of 'A' Flight after joining No 41 Sqn on 6 May 1917. Although he suffered minor injuries in a crash in FE 8 6408 on 11 June, he stayed in the squadron and was eventually credited with five victories in Airco DH 5s and three in SE 5as (*Aaron Weaver*)

On this occasion, however, the 'Red Baron's' revenge was administered by his 'gentlemen', Ltn Karl Schäfer shooting down 2Lt W B Hills in FE 8 6397 and 2Lt G F Heseler in A4874, while Ltn Kurt Wolff brought down Lt T Shepherd in 6456 – all three men became PoWs. FE 8 6399 was set afire by Ltn Karl Allmenröder, but its wounded pilot, 2Lt R E Neve, managed to jump just before the aircraft hit the ground near Hulluch, in Allied lines, and he was taken to hospital at Bethune.

In addition to those casualties, Lt W Morrice's FE 8 7636 came back with a jammed Lewis gun and enough damage to be written off, while 2Lt H C Todd landed at No 2 Sqn's field at Hesdigneul with 6425's aileron controls shot away and hits to his Lewis gun and airscrew. Todd nevertheless claimed an Albatros OOC.

On 12 March the first Nieuport 17s arrived at Treizennes, and No 40 Sqn quickly began transitioning to the newer fighters. Amid that, on the 19th, Benbow was wounded by anti-aircraft fire and posted out. He

would return to lead a flight as a captain in SE 5a-equipped No 85 Sqn in May 1918, but was killed without having added to his tally on the 30th of that month by Oblt Hans-Eberhardt Gandert of *Jasta* 51.

The FE 8s of No 41 Sqn soldiered on, three sharing their last victory over an Albatros two-seater on 16 June. On 11 July the unit began trading its FEs for DH 5s, and it did not truly come into its own until November 1917, when No 41 Sqn re-equipped with SE 5as.

A 'FEE' VC

Although its 250 hp Rolls-Royce Eagle engine gave it better performance than the Beardmore-powered FE 2b at altitudes of 5000 ft or higher, the FE 2d was still intrinsically easy meat for the Albatros-equipped *Jastas* that proliferated over the Western Front in 1917, culminating in the slaughter of 'Bloody April'. Yet their crews, by skill and teamwork – from the two men in the nacelle to mutually supporting formations – continued to work wonders in their big, hapless but far-from-helpless pushers.

Formed at Netheravon on 1 September 1915, No 20 Sqn began operations on FE 2bs in February 1916, before switching to FE 2ds five months later. Although it seemed to glory in its lack of distinctive markings (throughout its history, including its later period on Bristol F 2Bs, it was the drabbest looking British squadron on the Western Front), No 20 Sqn produced a galaxy of ace pilots and observers, and started 1917 off with a supreme act of valour.

Born in Widnes, Lancashire, on 17 January 1892, Thomas Mottershead had married Lilian Bree on 10 February 1914 and was a garage mechanic when war broke out. Enlisting in the RFC on 10 August, he was posted to the Central Flyng School at Upavon, where he rose in rank to sergeant on 1 April 1916. The following month Mottershead commenced flight training, which showed him to be as proficient a pilot as he had been a mechanic. After a short while spent as a flying instructor, he was posted to No 25 Sqn

Pilots and observers of No 20 Sqn in 1916. Standing, from left to right, are Lt Dennis, Lt D B Woolley (PoW 17 March 1917), 2Lt E D Spicer (KIA 1 February 1917) and 2Lt J T Gibbon (KIA 6 February 1917). Seated, from left to right, are Lt R B W Wainwright (three victories, WIA 15 February 1917), 2Lt C Gordon-Davis, Capt George Ranald Macfarlane Reid (nine victories, MC and Bar) and Lt R W White (two victories, injured in accident on 31 January 1917). Sitting in the front row, from left to right, are Lt W E Gower (WIA 7 January 1917) and 2Lt H R Wilkinson (three victories) (*Norman Franks*)

Shot down in flames by Vfw Walter Göttsch of *Jasta* 8 on 7 January 1917, Flt Sgt Thomas Mottershead of No 20 Sqn managed to coax FE 2d A'39 back to British lines before crash-landing. His efforts earned him a posthumous VC, as well as an MC for his observer, Lt W E Gower (*Norman Franks*)

on 6 July, where he soon established a reputation for being cool and courageous under fire.

Flying FE 2b 6998 on 22 September, Mottershead bombed an ammunition train at Samain railway station, and his observer, 2Lt C Street, strafed a second train along its length. As Mottershead pulled up, he was attacked from behind by a Fokker, but managed to turn the tables to allow Street to shoot it down. Awarded the DCM and promoted to flight sergeant, Mottershead was given two weeks' leave in England before returning to the front with No 20 Sqn.

On 7 January 1917 Mottershead took off in FE 2d A'39, with Lt W E Gower in the observer's pit, on a two-aeroplane patrol over Ploegsteert Wood. Soon after arriving over their assigned sector, the two FEs were attacked by a pair of Albatros scouts, which separated them. Gower's fire sent his antagonist spinning down, but seconds later the second Albatros, flown by Vfw Walter Göttsch of *Jasta* 8, got under A'39's tail and put a point-blank burst into the petrol tank.

With flames literally at his back, Mottershead dived for Allied lines while Gower played a hand-held fire extinguisher over him. Although they reached the British trenches, Mottershead, concerned for his observer's safety, postponed landing until he spotted a flat field. After circling and managing to touch down, A'39's undercarriage collapsed, throwing Gower clear but pinning Mottershead in the cockpit. Gower and nearby troops managed to extricate him from the wreckage and rushed him to the nearest medical centre, but Mottershead died of his burns and injuries on 12 January.

Gower was awarded the MC for his role in the drama. On 12 February Thomas Motterhead was posthumously gazetted for the VC, thus becoming the only non-commissioned airman in the RFC to receive Britain's highest military honour.

UNHAPPY VALENTINE'S DAY

Since his first double victory on 1 July 1916, Lt Harold Hartney had scored a third on 20 October in FE 2d A'30 with 2Lt W T Jourdan as his observer. After some leave time in England, he returned to No 20 Sqn in command of 'A' Flight and resumed his scoring on 2 February, when he and fellow Canadian 2Lt H R Wilkinson (in A1960, Hartney's ninth assigned FE 2d in eight months) downed a Halberstadt D II near Lille.

On 3 February 2Lt C Gordon-Davis and Capt R M Knowles, in A1962, claimed a 'Halbertadt OOC' over Wervicq. Their victim turned out to be Vfw Walter Göttsch, who since downing Mottershead on 7 January had destroyed two more No 20 Sqn FE 2ds on 1 February. His wounds kept him out of *Jasta* 8 until April, but No 20 Sqn had not seen the last of him.

Promoted to captain, Hartney was planning to lead a reconnaissance mission on the afternoon of 14 February when No 20 Sqn's CO, Maj W H C Mansfield, fresh from a visit to Army HQ in Cassel, took him to one side. 'You know Hartney, there's a push coming, and the brass hats over at GHQ are shy some photographs of the forest area around Passchendaele to complete their map of the whole enemy sector. I promised we'd get them today. You will take this mission, but at least one machine must accompany you as you cross the lines'.

FE 2d A'34 of No 20 Sqn was brought down at Roncq, southeast of Lille, on 25 January 1917. Although credited to Oblt Karl von Grieffenhagen of *Jasta* 18, it was also claimed by a flak unit. The wounded crewmen, Lts S Adler and R W White, were taken prisoner (*Jon Guttman*)

At 1400 hrs Hartney took off in A1960, with Jourdan in the observer's pit. Their escort, A'15, crewed by 2Lt F J Taylor and F M Myers, was late in taking off, but Hartney still managed to rendezvous with them over Ypres. Behind Taylor, however, Hartney spotted seven Albatros D IIIs descending on them from over Allied lines.

'I fairly danced with all my weight on the rudder bars', Hartney recalled, as his aeroplane skidded left and right in a descent toward home, followed by Taylor's. After dodging German attacks with a series of *renversements*, the two FEs began circling, their pilots trying to edge ever closer to home while their observers fired at targets of opportunity. 'Suddenly, as if on signal, the right rear enemy ship left the formation and took a swoop at us', Hartney wrote. 'His tracer bullets were playing around us for fully two seconds before Jourdan finally let him have both guns right in the face. The poor brave kid just kept on going, for all the world like a mortally wounded bird plummeting to his death near a river bend below us'.

Two more Albatros scouts dived on the FEs, but Hartney claimed that their observers shot both of them down, 'one bursting into flames and the other crashed to Eternity out of control in a slow but spinning dive'. The other four Germans had disappeared, but as the FEs headed for home, Hartney saw Taylor's aeroplane falter and break up in the air under fire

69

from what he took to be an eighth Albatros. Hartney turned and climbed to deal with Taylor's attacker, firing his own fixed Lewis gun but finding himself unable to aim because his aeroplane was stalling.

'Immediately, a terrific, almost unbelieveable, vibration took possession of my ship, like a train off the track bumping over the ties', Hartney continued. 'I tried to pull my throttle back slowly to dampen it out, but it only seemed to get worse. My switch would not cut the ignition'. He turned off the petrol flow and the FE began to spin earthward. At 6000 ft he began a gentle pullout, at which point he and Jourdan noticed that many of his flying wires were broken and one propeller blade had snapped off near the hub.

'I'll stretch my glide as far as I can', Hartney shouted, hoping to reach the trenches near Poperinghe. 'Don't crash her too hard', Jourdan replied calmly, stuffing photographic plates in his flight suit, 'I've got some good pictures here'.

Hartney made it over the lines, only to see one wing come down and his aeroplane crash in a Belgian field full of 15-ft hop poles! When he came to, he found himself pinned in the mud under his 775-lb motor, with Australian troops making an awkward extrication attempt that only caused the engine to fall back down on him. Jourdan, thrown from the aeroplane, was also injured, and ended up alongside Hartney in hospital. Taylor had also been injured crash landing in Allied lines and Myers was dead. Hartney, who was credited with his fifth and sixth victories in that fight, believed that he and Taylor were both victims of von Richthofen, but they were in fact credited to Ltn Paul Strähle (his first of 14 victories) and Uffz Flemming of *Jasta* 18, which, in spite of Hartney's perceptions, had lost no pilots of its own.

Hartney would later score a seventh victory with the USAS whilst serving as CO of the 27th Aero Squadron, and finished the war as a lieutenant colonel in command of the 1st Pursuit Group.

If the FE 2b reconnaissance units exhibited an attitude that their crews could take care of themselves if need be, and the FE 2d-equipped No 20 Sqn sallied forth with an almost aggressive élan, the FE 2b crews who concentrated on bombing accumulated their aerial tallies during the course of one running fight into and back from enemy territory after another. If their relatively large, tight, formations did not attract enemy attention, the commotion created by their bombing did, resulting in high odds on a return flight through a gauntlet of anti-aircraft artillery, sporadic ground fire and enemy fighters.

Inevitably, some pilots and observers accumulated enough victories to endow them (retrospectively) with ace status. The FE 2bs' often suffered horrific attrition during their bombing sorties, and a pilot or gunner surviving with five or more enemy aeroplanes to his credit was as much a reflection of endurance and sheer luck in cheating the law of averages as it was of skill.

One of No 18 Sqn's more successful pilots in 1917 was Victor Henry Huston, an Irishman who had emigrated to Canada before the war, but who went to France with the Canadian Expeditionary Force in 1915 and transferred to the RFC the following year. Joining No 18 Sqn in December, he scored the first of his six victories on 15 February 1917, when he and 2Lt P S Taylor destroyed a two-seater over Grevillers.

Canadian Lt Harold Evans Hartney flew FE 2ds with No 20 Sqn, and he had scored six victories by the time he was brought down wounded in British lines on 14 February 1917. He had almost certainly fallen victim to Ltn Paul Strähle of *Jasta* 18. Later joining the USAS, Maj Hartney scored a seventh victory in a Nieuport 28 while leading the 27th Aero Squadron in 1918, and he ended the war as a lieutenant colonel, commanding the 1st Pursuit Group (*Charles Woolley*)

Another expatriate was 2Lt James Robert Smith, who was born in the Isles of Orkney on 8 May 1891, but went off to Canada to work as an electrical and mechanical engineer in Prince Edward, Saskatchewan, from 1910 to 1912. He then ran his own business in Regina in 1913-14. Returning to the UK when war broke out, he served as an observer in No 18 Sqn and claimed his first Albatros D II on 26 December 1916, with 2Lt W F McDonald as his pilot. Flying with Lt H A R Boustead, Smith claimed two more Albatros D IIs on 11 March.

Relatively colourful among the 'Fee' units with its flight-signifying nacelle stripes, No 25 Sqn was also notable for constantly sallying forth into harm's way and suffering considerable losses for its trouble. Some of crews managed to claim a few back from the enemy, however.

Most notable among No 25 Sqn's early members was Lancelot Lytton Richardson, an Australian who had been born in Bereen Barraba, New South Wales, on 18 October 1895. After entering the RFC in January 1916 and joining No 25 Sqn on 3 June, he scored his first victory over a Fokker E III in concert with observer Lt M V Lewes and two other crews on 17 June. For his second success, again over a Fokker, Richardson teamed up with future observer ace 2AM Leslie Simpson Court.

Richardson and Lewes forced an Albatros two-seater to land on 2 July, while Court, in company with Capt M C B Copeman, downed a Fokker on the 15th. On 20 July Richardson and Court claimed two Fokkers, but their FE 2b (6932) was shot up and Richardson wounded. Returning early in 1917 as a flight leader, Capt Richardson re-opened his account with a two-seater with Lt W G Meggitt on 15 February and an Albatros D II with 2Lt Douglas Charles Wollen on 17 March.

While Richardson was recuperating, Court served as observer for the newly arrived Cpl Thomas Mottershead during his familiarisation flights and initial combat sorties. On 5 August Court and 2Lt W H Rilett were brought down just behind the trenches and their aeroplane (4922) shelled. Teamed with 2Lt Noel W W Webb in 6993, Court brought down a two-seater OOC on 9 September and, after being promoted to sergeant, he and 2Lt V W Harrison claimed another two-seater on the 27th, although on the latter occasion they were in turn brought down by their opponents, Ltn Albert Dossenbach and Oblt Hans Schilling of *Fl Abt* 22 – all four combatants survived the experience.

With 2Lt James L Leith as his pilot, Court was credited with a scout destroyed on 22 October and a Fokker biplane scout OOC on 9 November, bringing his final tally to eight. Although curiously unrecognised by his own service, Court was awarded the *Médaille Militaire* by the French on 1 May 1917.

Court's penultimate victory was the first for one of No 25 Sqn's future top pilots. Born in London on 20 December 1896, James Leith started the war in the Hampshire Regiment, but joined the RFC in February 1916. Leith's second success was Court's last, on 9 November 1916. He and 2Lt A G Servers then downed an Albatros D II on 24 January 1917, and he got another with 2Lt Wollen as his observer five days later. Promoted to captain and flight leader, Leith scored his fifth victory (another D II) on 1 March with Lt G M A Hobart-Hampden, and another on 17 March was shared by him and future observer ace 2AM Leonard H Emsden.

Another successful pilot in No 25 Sqn was Canadian Reginald George Malcolm, who was born in Manitoba in 1890. His first victory – an Albatros D III shared with three other FE 2bs on 4 March – was also the first for 2AM Emsden. Both men were up, albeit in separate aircraft, on the morning of 17 March when Malcolm and Lt C W Wilson claimed an Albatros D III while Emsden, with Lt H E Davis as his pilot, was credited with one in flames, followed by another OOC that same afternoon with Capt Leith in the pilot's seat.

—————— 'FEES' 'BLOODY APRIL' ——————

April 1917 saw the launching of a new Allied offensive, conceived by French General Robert Nivelle, which was executed awkwardly from the start. The British offensive, intened to support Nivelle's, actually starting earlier, on 9 April, while the French one got belatedly underway on the 16th, culminating in the Second Battle of the Aisne. Aside from the Canadian seizure of Vimy Ridge, the push ended in general disappointment on the ground. In the air, the RFC and RNAS lost three times as many aircraft as the Germans, thanks primarily to the deadly efficiency of the *Jagdstaffeln* in a month that the British came to call 'Bloody April'.

The FE units were hit particularly hard, as they saw considerable action against foes flying aircraft that had a much better performance than anything they had battled the year before. The month got off to a bad start when a machine from No 22 Sqn and two from No 57 Sqn were lost on 2 April, the latter two falling to Vfw Sebastian Festner and Ltn Konstantin Krefft of Manfred von Richthofen's *Jasta* 11. Of three lost the next day, two from No 25 Sqn fell to Ltn Karl Emil Schäfer and to Oblt von Richthofen himself.

On 5 April, the first combat sortie by Bristol F 2A Fighters of No 48 Sqn ended in disaster as four out of the first six-aeroplane flight were shot down by *Jasta* 11, two by von Richthofen. The flight leader, Capt

FE 2b A5478 *GOLD COAST No 10* was delivered to No 23 Sqn in February 1917. Two months later the unit transitioned to SPAD VIIs, so the aircraft was transferred to No 100 Sqn, with whom it flew night bombing missions – often with Lt Henry 'Jack' Morley as the pilot – until stricken off charge on 18 August. After becoming outdated as reconnaissance fighters, many FEs served on as night bombers well into 1918, their nocturnal raids often continuing to take a toll on German *Jagstaffeln* at their own aerodromes (*Henry Morley album via Jon Guttman*)

Born on 16 April 1895 in Leoville, Ireland, Giles Noble Blennerhasset served in the 4th Royal Irish Rifles prior to joining the RFC on 24 March 1916 and being assigned as an observer to No 18 Sqn on 31 December. With 2Lt Victor H Huston as his pilot in FE 2b 4969 on 5 April 1917, 2Lt Blennerhasset downed two Albatros D IIs over Inchy. Two D IIIs on 23 May, with 2Lt D Marshall as his pilot, brought his total to eight. Posted to HE on 19 July, Blennerhasset was awarded the MC one week later and subsequently qualified as a pilot, serving in Nos 78, 112, 153 and 39 HD Sqns. After postwar service in India, Blennerhasset resigned his RAF commission on 22 January 1922. He passed away in December 1978 (*Norman Franks*)

William Leefe Robinson VC, was captured after being brought down by Ltn Kurt Wolff. It proved to be a deceptively inauspicious debut for what would soon prove to be one of the war's best fighting aircraft, the F 2 Fighter soon eclipsing the FE 2d in the two-seat fighter role.

Ironically, the 5th also saw the Germans reminded that however obsolescent they were becoming, FEs were not helpless, and their crews could still occasionally draw blood. During a running fight with nine Albatros D IIIs of *Jasta* 18, Capt G J Mahoney-Jones and Capt R M Knowles of No 20 Sqn sent two opponents down OOC over Courtrai and Houthulst. Nearby, 2Lt J Lawson and Sgt Clayton were badly shot up but made it back to Abeele, having been claimed by – but not confirmed to – Ltn Ernst Wiessner.

That same day, 2Lt H G White and Pte T E Allum (in FE 2d A6385) fought off two more D IIIs. Allum, on his first mission, was not up to the job, so White fired the rear Lewis gun himself whenever an overshooting attacker presented him with a target. A lucky shot brought down D III 1942/16 in Allied lines, where the pilot, Ltn Josef Flink of *Jasta* 18, was taken prisoner with a bad hand wound, while White and Allum came home feeling both relieved and pleased with themselves.

Born in Maidstone, Kent, on 1 March 1898, Hugh Granville White had contemplated a naval career, but attended the Royal Military College at Sandhurst instead and was commissioned in the East Kent Regiment, before joining the RFC in early 1916. He was still 17 when he arrived at No 20 Sqn in July of that same year, earning him the nickname 'Child Pilot'. Despite his youth, White would claim two more victories on 23 and 26 May, flying FE 2d A6512 with 2Lt T A M S Lewis as his observer, to add to his success on 5 April. He had become a flight commander by the time he returned to Home Establishment (HE), aged 18.

Later leading an SE 5a flight in No 29 Sqn, White scored four more victories in May 1918, the last of which involved him surviving a collision with a Pfalz D IIIa that killed his less fortunate opponent, Vfw Karl Pech of *Jasta* 29. Rising to the rank of air vice marshal in a career that included service in the RAF's rugby team prior to his retirement in 1955, White died on 23 September 1983.

Also active on 5 April 1917 was No 23 Sqn, which lost an FE 2d to Ltn d R Georg Schlenker of *Jasta* 3, and No 18 Sqn, one of whose FE 2bs was on a photo-reconnaissance mission for the Fifth Army when it was claimed by Ltn d R Friedrich Roth of *Jasta* 12 over Gouzeaucourt at 1105 hrs. The mortally wounded pilot of the latter aircraft actually managed to come down in British lines near Bapaume prior to passing away. During a subsequent, equally contested, mission 2Lt Victor Huston of No 18 Sqn and 21-year-old 2Lt Giles Noble Blennerhasset from Leoville, in Ireland, claimed two Albatros D IIs over Inchy at 1200 hrs – Blennerhasset had scored a previous victory back on 4 February. Another Albatros was credited as OOC to 2Lt James Smith, flying in FE 2b A6464, with Capt R H Hood as his pilot.

By 1917, everyone may have been well past seeing any irony in 6 April – Good Friday and, coincidentally the day the United States declared war on Germany – for it brought yet more frenetic aerial activity and heavy losses on both sides. The Germans claimed no less than nine FEs that day, of which six were actually shot down. Four of them were lost by 'A' Flight of No 57 Sqn, which, led by Capt A C Wright, had generated a six-aeroplane offensive patrol from Fienvillers aerodrome at 0700 hrs. One FE 2d left the formation with engine trouble at 0820 hrs, and soon afterwards Wright and Pte R Sibley attacked a two-seater and drove it down, but not before its observer had wounded the former in the knee.

Wright's flight then came under a rapid succession of attacks by *Jastas* 12, 'Boelcke' and 5, whose pilots claimed a total of five victories. Four of the FE 2ds came down behind German lines, their crews being taken prisoner. Wright's aeroplane was hit in the radiator and his motor soon seized up, but he made a four-mile glide for home, protected from the bullets of his pusruers by the dead engine behind him. Ground fire struck him in the thigh, but Wright made it over the frontlines and force-landed 50 yards from some Australian outposts.

The CO's demise was credited to *Jasta* 12's commander, Hptm Paul von Osterroht, but Wright and his flight had made the Germans pay for their success. During the course of bringing down one of the FEs, Ltn Otto Splitgerber of *Jasta* 12 was himself wounded and forced to disengage. Worse still for *Jasta* 5, in the midst of the melee its *Staffelführer*, ten-victory ace Oblt Hans Berr, collided with Vfw Paul Hoppe and both men fell to their deaths.

At the same time that No 57 Sqn was fighting for its survival, four FE 2bs from No 22 Sqn came under attack from seven enemy fighters as they attempted to carry out a photo-reconnaissance mission southeast of Gouy. The crews fought their way out, with one German scout being credited as forced to land near Lesdins and another destroyed by all four aeroplanes, whose crews included the future ace teams of Capt Carleton Main Clement/2Lt Llewelyn C Davies and Lt John V Aspinall/2Lt Medley K Parlee. The victim of their crossfire may have been Vfw Reinhold Wurzmann of *Jasta* 20, who fell in flames near Marcy, east of St Quentin.

Two hours later, ten FE 2ds from No 20 Sqn were en route to bomb Ledeghem when they were intercepted by *Jasta* 8 at 1000 hrs. In the running fight that ensued, 2Lts E J Smart and H N Hampson were credited with a Halberstadt destroyed and two OOC, while 2Lt E O Perry and Pte Allum forced a fourth to crash land in a field. On the debit side, Smart and Hampson's FE (A'3) was damaged and had to force land in British lines, a second riddled aeroplane landed at Bailleul airfield, an observer was wounded and FE 2d A6358 was shot down over Polygon Wood, its crew, 2Lt R Smith and Lt R Hume, being killed. They were credited to Offstv Walter Göttsch, back from hospital and destined to meet his old enemies at No 20 Sqn again before the month was out.

While on a photo-reconnaissance mission over Farbus Wood that eventful morning, FE 2bs of No 25 Sqn came under attack by 14 Albatros and Halberstadt scouts. For a change, the long-suffering squadron managed to fight its way home with only one shot-up aeroplane, crewed by 2Lt R G Malcolm and Lt D E Holmes, which force-landed near the British 9th Kite Balloon Section at Bray.

No 25 Sqn had even managed to claimed two victories, the first of which fell to 2Lts Alexander Roulstone and E G Green when they destroyed an Albatros D III that they had seen down a BE 2c of No 16 Sqn in flames over Givency at 1030 hrs. Their victim was apparently Ltn

Schäfer of *Jasta* 11, who actually survived the encounter unhurt, although he would later tangle with one FE too many. Fifteen minutes later, 2Lt B King and Cpl L H Emsden claimed a Halberstadt east of Vimy.

After five days of little aerial action for the 'Fee' units, on 11 April No 18 Sqn's observer ace 2Lt James Smith came back with a serious stomach wound and was invalided to England. Strangely, the Germans claimed no FEs on this date. Awarded the *Croix de Guerre* with *Palme* by the French on 14 July, Smith subsequently served in three Home Defence units (Nos 33, 51 and 78), before returning to Canada at the end of 1919.

The Germans claimed nine FEs on 13 April, of which five were actually lost – three of them from No 25 Sqn. The first, claimed by Ltn Hans Klein of *Jasta* 4 at 1910 hrs, killed two of the unit's best men, Capt Lancelot Richardson, who was posthumously awarded the MC a month later, and Lt Douglas Wollen.

Meanwhile, at 1840 hrs Capt Leith, who would also soon be awarded the MC, was leading six FE 2bs on a mission to bomb an ammunition dump at the railway junction between Hénin-Liétard and Lens. At 1930 hrs, however, the FEs encountered five Albatros D IIIs, which suddenly dived on two of Leith's flight and knocked out their engines, sending both down. Leith, with observer Lt Hobart-Hampden, accompanied by another FE crewed by Sgts W J Burtenshaw and J R Brown, turned to aid the the stricken machines, and in the fight that ensued the crews claimed an Albatros each, with a third being credited to 2Lt Malcolm and Cpl Emsden. The squadron lost both of the aeroplanes that had fallen victim to that first enemy attack, however, and their assailants, from *Jasta* 11, actually suffered no casualties. Sgt J Dempsey and his wounded observer, Lt W H Green, were captured, their demise being credited to Vfw Festner, while 2Lt Allan Harold Bates and Sgt William Alfred Barnes had been killed by Rittm Manfred von Richthofen.

The next notable clash involving FEs occurred on 21 April, when *Jasta* 30 took on No 25 Sqn and their escorting Sopwith Triplanes of No 8 Sqn RNAS. Coming under attack, Lt Reginald Malcolm and 2Lt J B Weir returned fire and hit their assailant, who was finished off by Flt Sub-Lt Antony Rex Arnold of 'Naval 8'. Their victim, Ltn Gustav Nernst, crashed to his death in Allied lines, where his Albatros D III (2147/16) was recovered and given the captured aircraft classification G22 by the British. Another D III was credited as OOC to Capt Leith and Lt Hobart-Hampden.

Posted out for a rest in May, Leith would return to the front flying Sopwith Camels as a flight leader in No 46 Sqn, scoring his ninth, and final, victory on 2 October when he, Capt Donald R MacLaren and Lt C H Sawyer sent a Fokker D VII down OOC over Morcourt.

Von Richthofen downed another FE 2b on 22 April, this time from No 11 Sqn, while a second fell to his *Staffel* mate Ltn Kurt Wolff. The next day saw Ltn Kurt Schneider of *Jasta* 5 credited with two FE 2bs and Ltn Hermann Göring of *Jasta* 27 claim one, but this time all of their victims seem to have come down alive in Allied lines.

While escorting Sopwith 1¹/2 Strutters of No 45 Sqn on a photo-reconnaissance mission on 24 April, six of No 20 Sqn's FE 2ds got into a scrap with 18 Albatros scouts from *Jastas* 8 and 18, as well as *Marine Feld Jasta* 1, west of Ledeghem at 0729 hrs. Offstv Göttsch and Ltn Werner

Junck of *Jasta* 8 claimed an FE apiece, the latter's victory resulting in the deaths of 2Lt A R Johnston and Lt W R Nicholson – Göttch's quarry reached Allied lines before force landing. In return, Lts R E Johnson and F R Cubbon claimed two of the Germans destroyed, one of whom was the CO of *Jasta* 18, Rittm Karl von Grieffenhagen. Badly injured when he crash-landed, von Grieffenhagen lost a leg and part of his lower jaw.

As the fighting retreat continued, with *Jasta* 18 to the fore, Ltn Walter von Bülow-Bothkamp set FE 2d A5144 on fire, but its wounded pilot, Lt N L Robertson, brought his machine down in Allied lines near Ypres, with his observer, Capt R M Knowles, only lightly wounded. Although also set on fire, 2Lt Perry got his FE to Allied territory too. He and his observer, 2AM Edward Harper Sayers from Merton, South London, sent an Albatros down in flames during their fighting retreat, its pilot, Ltn Fritz Kleindienst, jumping to his death north of Comines. Also lost was Vzflgmstr Josef Wirtz, who was credited with two FE 2ds destroyed before allegedly colliding with one of them and crashing to his death over Polygon Wood.

Also active on the 24th was No 18 Sqn, which claimed three Albatros D IIIs destroyed – one in flames – over Barelle. One of these victories was credited to Lts V H Huston and E A Foord, who had downed Offstv Rudolf Weckbrodt of *Jasta* 26. The latter was wounded in the clash, but he had rejoined his unit by month-end. Huston and Foord would be credited with a Halberstadt on 13 May, and exactly two weeks later they shared in the destruction of an Albatros D V north of Havrincourt with a Pup flown by Flt Sub-Lt H S Kerby of No 3 Sqn RNAS. Awarded the MC on 16 June, Victor Huston subsequently served as an instructor for the Chilean Air Force, having retired from the RAF in November 1919.

Returning to 24 April, during a scrap at 1750 hrs, Lt Roulstone and 2Lt Green of No 25 Sqn were credited with an Albatros D III destroyed over Billy-Montingny. Roulstone would score once more in an FE 2b on 21 May, and add another three to his tally in DH 4s by 22 August. Awarded the MC and returning to the front as a flight leader in No 57 Sqn, Roulstone would score twice more in DH 4s before he was wounded on 17 March 1918 – but not before he and his observer, 2Lt V C Venmore, had killed their assailant, *Jasta* 30 CO and 20-victory ace Oblt Hans Bethge.

The 25th saw another No 25 Sqn FE 2b crew killed by Schäfer of *Jasta* 11 and a second damaged aeroplane force landing in Allied lines. On the 26th ten FE 2ds of No 20 Sqn, carrying two 112-lb bombs apiece, attacked Rumbeke aerodrome, where they incurred the wrath of eight Albatros D IIIs from resident *Jasta* 8. The FE crews claimed two scouts out of control, while one RFC machine had to force-land in Allied lines near Watou, its observer, Sgt A Clayton, having been mortally wounded in the chest. In the second of two sorties that day No 22 Sqn fared worse, losing two crews (all PoWs) to Offstv Alfred Sturm and Ltn d R Rudolf Nebel of *Jasta* 5. No 11 Sqn lost two crews (again all PoWs) to *Jasta* 11 on the 27th courtesy of Ltns Lothar von Richthofen and Kurt Wolff.

Sunday, 29 April 1917 saw Manfred von Richthofen reach his personal career peak with four victories, including an FE 2b for his 50th, killing Sgt George Stead and Cpl Alfred Beebee of No 18 Sqn. Ltn Wolff claimed another, whose wounded crew made it to Allied lines. No 18 Sqn claimed three Albatros victories, but *Jasta* 11 suffered no casualties.

The top-scoring pusher pilot of World War 1, Capt Frederick James Henry Thayre was credited with 20 victories, mostly in FE 2d A6430 of No 20 Sqn (*Norman Franks*)

Capt Francis Richard Cubbon scored most of his 21 victories as Thayre's observer (*Norman Franks*)

At 1545 hrs, No 20 Sqn sent out a second formation from Abeele to bomb the ammunition dump at Bisseghem, and *Jasta* 18 scrambled up from Halluin to intercept the FEs west of Courtrai. In the ensuing melée the RFC crews claimed four Albatros – two in flames by Capt F H Thayre and Lt F R Cubbon, one crashed by 2Lt E J Smart and Lt T A M S Lewis and another OOC by Lt R E Conder and 2Lt H G Neville.

Jasta 18 recorded no personnel lost, while crediting FEs to Ltns Strähle, Wiessner and Gustav Nolte. Sgt S Attwater, Lt J E Davies and Lts V L A Burns and D L Houghton were brought down, all to become PoWs. Nolte claimed that his victim crashed in British lines near Hooge. A'29's crewmen, Perry and Allum – the latter credited with at least two more victories since 5 April, and promoted to 2AM – were wounded, but Perry managed to land and they got clear before their FE burnt out. A fourth machine, its fuel tank holed, landed at No 42 Sqn's Bailleul base.

It was No 57 Sqn's turn to suffer on 30 April, losing two aeroplanes to Lothar von Richthofen of *Jasta* 11 and Oblt Adolf Ritter von Tutschek of *Jasta* 12. A third FE 2d – A1966, crewed by Lts C S Morice and Forde Leathley – was pursued by Ltn Heinz Geiseler of *Jasta* 33 until forced to land near Roclincourt in Allied lines, its engine having seized from a holed radiator. Although they were not officially credited to Geiseler, Morice and Leathley were themsevles credited with an Albatros OOC. The 20-year-old Leathley, from Trillick, in Ireland, later added seven Albatros D Vs to his score in DH 4s, with Maj E G Joy as his pilot. He was awarded the MC for his success, and on 26 November 1917 earned his own pilot's certificate.

So ended what for the FEs had been an April of mixed fortunes, most of them indeed 'bloody'. And yet their daylight operations, like it or not, was not quite over. More remarkably, the next two months would show that these long-outdated two-seat pushers – especially the FE 2ds of No 20 Sqn – still had a last hurrah to sound.

TOP 'FEE' TEAM

It would be impossible to give details on all the pilots and observers who 'made ace' during the FE 2d's last few months with No 20 Sqn – the unit claimed 40 victories in May alone! As was the case with bombers and formations of one or more reconnaissance aeroplanes, FE victories were often shared, not only between pilot and observer but among the aeroplanes in the formation. Indeed, their very survival, let alone success, depended as much upon the coordinated sprays of lead these mutually supporting teams spewed forth as it did on one observer's marksmanship or luck.

An exceptional case, both statistically and in terms of how few of its victories were shared with others, was the team of Thayre and Cubbon, the most successful, and yet among the shortest-lived, of the FE 2 crews.

Frederick James Henry Thayre was born in London on 20 October 1894, but lived in Littlehampton before the war. Qualifying as a pilot in May 1915, he first served in No 16 Sqn, and it was while flying one of that unit's vulnerable BE 2cs that his observer, Lt C R Davidson, managed to shoot down an attacking Fokker E III on 18 March 1916. Thayre was later posted to No 20 Sqn, where he forged a formidable triumvirate with Lt F R Cubbon and FE 2d A6430.

Also born in London, on 26 November 1892, Francis Richard Cubbon spent most of his pre-war years living in Poona, India. When war broke out he enlisted in the Yorks and Lancs Regiment, and also served in the 72nd Punjabi and Royal Warwickshire regiments, before transferring to the RFC in October 1916. On 25 March 1917 Cubbon became an officer observer and joined No 20 Sqn in April. While flying with Lt R E Johnson in FE 2d A6392 on 24 March, Cubbon destroyed an Albatros D III and drove another down OOC west of Ledeghem. After that he teamed up with Lt Thayre in A6430 for what would prove to be the rest of their brief lives, and they started with the two 'flamers' on 29 April.

On 1 May Thayre and Cubbon shot an Albatros two-seater down in flames over Ploegsteert Wood, killing Uffz Karl Gottwald and Ltn Erich Heckmann of *Fl Abt* 6. After forcing a two-seater to land on 3 May (which was not counted in their score) the duo came under attack from 26 Albatros D IIIs, two of which they shot down over Moorlede and Westroosebeke. At a late stage in this fighting retreat they ran out of Lewis ammunition, and they were forced to fend off their attackers with their automatic pistols until the Germans finally disengaged.

During a fight between No 20 Sqn and *Jasta* 8 on 5 May, Ltn Göttsch brought down FE 2d A1942, whose pilot, a wounded 2Lt L G Bacon, became a PoW, but whose observer, 2AM G Worthing, was killed. Ltn Wiessner and Vfw Flemming were also credited with FEs, but the only other casualty suffered by No 20 Sqn was A5147, which made Allied territory despite being shot up. Its crew, 2Lts G C Heseltine and F J Kydd, escaped unhurt, having claimed two Alba-

Five-victory ace Capt Frank Douglas Stevens (left) and Lt William C Cambray pose with their FE 2d A6516, bearing the legend PRESENTED BY THE COLONY OF MAURITIUS *No 13*, at No 20 Sqn's aerodrome at Clairmarais in July 1917. Stevens claimed four of his victories in this machine, which was also piloted with some success by Lt H G E Luchford, with 2Lt James Tennant, 2Lt W D Kennard, Lt Frederick J Kydd and Lt Archibald N Jenks among its observers. A6516 was finally stricken off the rolls after suffering combat damage on 20 September (*Phil Jarrett*)

2Lt Richard Michael Trevethan whimsically models the fleece-lined 'fug boots' developed by Maj Lanoe G Hawker to help protect his DH 2 pilots – and all pusher crews, for that matter – from the muscle-numbing cold of high altitudes. A British citizen, although born in the United States on 24 January 1895, Trevethan was credited with 12 victories, ending with a 'double' on 8 August (*Norman Franks*)

tros, one of which they shared among the three credited to Thayre and Cubbon. Another fell to 2Lt R E Conder and 2AM J J Cowell in A6400. Of the total of nine D IIIs credited to No 20 Sqn's crews, one, destroyed over Houthem, cost *Jasta* 8 the life of Vfw Peter Glasmacher.

Frederick Joseph Kydd, born in Frodsham, Cheshire, on 15 May 1892, had been a medical student at Liverpool University until August 1914. He had served in the King's Liverpool Regiment prior to joining No 20 Sqn just two days before opening his account with Heseltine! Kydd would score thrice more, with 2Lt H B Howe on 9 May, with Lt Arthur Norbury Solly on 12 June and with Capt Frank D Stevens on 3

July, before being posted to HE on 11 August and serving as an instructor at No 1 School of Armament from July 1918 to 2 February 1919.

The German credited to 2Lt Reginald Edward Conder was his second victory of six prior to being wounded on 6 June – in error by British anti-

Lt Campbell Alexander Hoy, who had served in the Northern Cyclist Battalion, Territorial Force, before joining the RFC, had been injured on 25 May 1917 when FE 2d A6366 was shot down in Allied lines by Ltn August Hanko of *Jasta* 28 – his pilot, 2Lt Baring-Gould, was also wounded. Hoy was eventually credited with ten victories, eight of which were scored with Capt R M Trevethan as his pilot (*Norman Franks*)

Londoner 2Lt Oliver Henry Douglas Vickers of No 20 Sqn was 19 when he downed an Albatros D V with the aid of his Irish observer – and future 16-victory ace – Sgt John J Cowell on 29 June 1917. Mostly flying FE 2d A6376, Capt Vickers eventually became a flight leader and brought his total to 13 with four D Vs driven down OOC over Halluin in concert with Lt J A Hone on 17 August (*Norman Franks*)

Capt Stevens and Lt Cambray are seen in the cockpit of their FE 2d A6516. Worthy of note is the third Lewis gun fixed to the right side of the nacelle, which was an expedient adopted by several pilots in No 20 Sqn. A plate camera is also fitted to the left of the nacelle (*Phil Jarrett*)

aircraft fire. It was also the first for John J Cowell from County Limerick, who had joined the squadron in April and would subsequently fly with such crack pilots as 2Lt Richard Michael Trevethan, 2Lt Oliver Henry Douglas Vickers and Lt Cecil Roy Richards, in the process earning the DCM, MM and Bar. A year after scoring his 15th victory on 28 July, and being posted to HE, Cowell returned to No 20 Sqn as a Bristol F 2B pilot, teaming up with Cpl C Hill to down a Fokker D VII OOC on 29 July 1918. Both men were killed the next day, however, shot down by Ltn Fritz Röth of *Jasta* 16b.

Born on 24 July 1893, Australian 2Lt Cecil Roy Richards opened his account with an Albatros D III on 14 June 1917, and was eventually credited with 12 victories. Nine of these (including the first, as well as four Albatros D Vs on 17 July) were scored in concert with observer Lt Albert Edward Wear. Richards was gazetted for the MC, but on 19 August, three days after scoring his last victory, he and 2Lt C F Thompson were brought down wounded by Ltn Ernst Hess of *Jasta* 28 and taken PoW. Richards died at Glenelg, in South Australia, on 28 March 1973 (*Norman Franks*)

Thayre and Cubbon added steadily to their tally during May, with an Albatros D III on the 12th, followed by 'doubles' on the 13th, 23rd and 25th. Cubbon was promoted to captain, and both men received the MC and Bar. They finished the month by destroying a two-seater and a D III on the 27th.

Fighting continued almost daily throughout June as Lt Gen Herbert C O Plumer's Second Army prepared to launch its assault on Messines Ridge. On the morning of 5 June a patrol from No 22 Sqn was

Carleton Main Clement was attending Toronto University when war broke out, and he initially served in the 47th Battalion, Canadian Expeditionary Force, prior to joining the RFC. As a pilot in No 22 Sqn, he was credited with eight victories in FE 2bs and six more in Bristol F 2Bs, but on 19 August 1917 he and his observer, Lt R B Carter, were killed when shot down near Langemarck by *Flakzug* 99 (*Norman Franks*)

beset by Albatros D IIIs of *Jasta* 5, with FE 2b A857 being forced down intact at Vaucelles, where its wounded crew, Capt F P Don and 2Lt H Harris, were taken prisoner. Their loss was quickly avenged by 21-year-old Canadian Capt C M Clement and his Glaswegian observer, 2Lt Llewellyn Crichton Davies, in FE 2b A5461. They claimed two D IIIs northwest of Lesdains, with one of their victims being *Jasta* 5's acting CO, and 15-victory ace, Ltn Kurt Schneider, who suffered a severe thigh wound that became infected, resulting in his death on 14 July.

The morning's bag brought Davies' tally to five, for which he received the MC. Later serving in DH 4s with No 105 Sqn, he was severely injured in a crash on 13 March 1918 and died three days later. Clement, whose score now stood at eight, would claim another six in Bristol F 2Bs before he and his observer, Lt R B Carter, were killed by flak on 19 August 1918.

The Germans lost a second ace to a 'Fee' that day, as described by H A Jones in *The War in the Air* Vol IV;

'During the afternoon of the 5th, a formation of seven FE 2ds from No 20 Sqn had a running fight with about fifteen Albatros scouts over the Ypres-Menin road. The German leader, in a red Albatros, early attacked

2Lt Thomas Archibald Mitford Stewart Lewis was observer for Lt Harold Leslie Satchell when they shot down Ltn Karl-Emil Schäfer of *Jasta* 28 on 5 June 1917 (*Norman Franks*)

Ltn Karl-Emil Schäfer poses before his Albatros D III at the time he left *Jasta* 11 to take command of *Jasta* 28. What looks like a subtle change of dark shades just ahead of the fuselage cross suggests that Schäfer had retained his personal marking of a black fuselage after section and tail, but painted the rest of the fuselage, struts and wheels in *Jasta* 11 red. British descriptions of his last combat suggest that his aeroplane was all – or mostly – red on 5 June 1917. The 30-victory ace, and commander of Württemberg *Jasta* 28, had amassed the majority of victories flying under von Richthofen in *Jasta* 11 during 'Bloody April'. On 5 June 1917, Schäfer led *Jasta* 28 in an attack on seven FE 2ds of No 20 Sqn. He was shot down by Lt H L Stachell and his observer, 2Lt T A M S Lewis, in FE 2d A6469 (*Greg VanWyngarden*)

one of the FEs and mortally wounded its pilot, Lt W W Sawden, who dived for home, closely pursued by the Albatros.

'Another of the FE 2ds (pilot Lt H L Satchell and observer 2Lt T A M S Lewis) went to the assistance of Lt Sawden and engaged the red Albatros in a combat lasting 15 minutes. The German pilot showed exceptional skill and tenacity, but, eventually, a burst of bullets from the FE 2d at very close range shattered a part of the Albatros, which broke up in the air and crashed near Zandvoorde. The pilot proved to be Ltn Karl Schäfer, one of the foremost German fighting pilots who had, at the time of his death, 30 Allied aeroplanes to his credit.'

In addition to Satchell's and Lewis' victory in FE 2d A6469, an Albatros D III was credited to Thayre and Cubbon, and another downed over Coucou was the fourth credited to both Capt Donald Charles Cunnell and his observer, Sgt E H Sayers.

In his combat report, in which he claimed both he and Lewis were firing at their assailant, Lt Harold Leslie Satchell stated, 'Eventually, after

German troops look over the remains of Schäfer's Albatros D III after his fatal encounter with No 20 Sqn (*Greg VanWyngarden*)

81

a long burst of fire at very close range, the red hostile aircraft burst into flames and all its wings fell off. This hostile aircraft crashed near Becelaere'. Although the same entry appeared in Satchell's logbook, nobody else seems to have seen Schäfer go down in flames, including Offstv Max Müller of *Jasta* 28, who claimed to have seen the Albatros break up and crash vertically. Photographs of the crash show neither evidence of burning nor that all the wings came off.

Satchell's observer, Thomas Archibald Mitford Stewart Lewis, was born in Edenbridge, Kent, on 26 June 1894, and served with the Royal West Kent Regiment, Territorial Force, before transferring to the RFC in October 1916. He had downed his first Albatros D III on 29 April with 2Lt E J Smart, and two more with 'Child Pilot' H G White in May. Two Albatros D Vs downed with 2Lt G T Burkett in A6512 on 27 July brought Lewis' total to six, for which he received the MC. He died on 21 June 1961.

On 7 June 1917 the Battle of Messines commenced with a bang – from 19 mines laid under the German trenches by British sappers – and that evening Capts Thayre and Cubbon sent an Albatros down shedding its wings over Houthem. Their victim was a frequently encountered adversary of No 20 Sqn, Ltn Ernst Wiessner of *Jasta* 18, who had just downed an RE 8 for his fifth victory earlier that day. It was Thayre's 20th victory and Cubbon's 21st.

Two days later, the highest scoring FE crew was leading an offensive patrol when it spotted an Albatros two-seater east of Ploegsteert. Thayre dived, Cubbon fired and the German aircraft was last seen in a vertical nose dive streaming smoke, but nobody observed it crash. Just as Thayre was pulling up to rejoin his flight, A6430 suddenly took a direct shell hit from *K Flak* 60 and crashed hear Warneton. The Germans subsequently dropped a message confirming the crew's demise, but their graves were never found. On 18 July Cubbon's MC and Bar were gazetted, although he had already received them on 11 and 16 May.

Four days after the loss of Thayre and Cubbon, another great two-seater pilot opened his account in the FE 2d when Lt Henry George

Nicknamed 'Child Pilot' when he joined No 20 Sqn in July 1916, 17-year-old 2Lt Hugh Granville White soon earned a flight command. He scored his first victory, with Pte T E Allum, on 5 April 1917, resulting in Albatros D III 1942/16 and its pilot, Ltn Josef Flink of *Jasta* 18, falling into Allied hands. White scored two more victories with 2Lt T A M S Lewis on 23 and 26 May, and got four more in SE 5as with No 29 Sqn in May 1918. Retiring as an air vice marshal in 1955, White died on 23 September 1983 (*Jack Eder via Jon Guttman*)

FE 2d A6548 of No 20 Sqn was used by 24-victory ace H G E Luchford (with observer Lt M W Waddington) to claim his sixth and seventh successes – both Albatros D IIIs OOC – on 17 and 21 July 1917 (*A Weaver*)

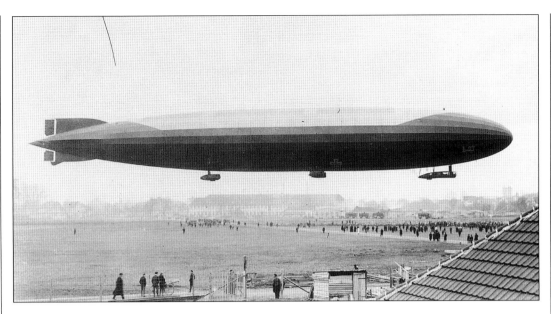

L43 was one of the new generation of Zeppelins that were dubbed 'height climbers' by the British, as they sought safety from interception and flak by ascending to high altitude. On 14 June 1917, *L43* was shot down by a Curtiss H 12 flying boat of the Royal Navy. Three nights later, a series of unfortunate events led to its sister-ship, *L48*, suffering an even more embarrassing demise at the hands of long-obsolete pusher aeroplanes (*Jon Guttman*)

Ernest Luchford and 2Lt James Tennant drove an Albatros D III down OOC over Houthem. Harry Luchford, 23, was working as a bank clerk in Bromley, Kent, when war broke out. Subsequently soldiering in the Norfolk Regiment, the Army Service Corps and the Indian Cavalry Division, prior to joining the RFC in January 1916, he qualified as a pilot and joined No 20 Sqn in May. Coincidentally, 21-year-old Tennant, from Newton Stewart, in Scotland, had also been a banker pre-war.

Luchford's next victory came at 1310 hrs on 29 June, with 2Lt W D Kennard in the observer's pit. Four FE 2ds, having dropped some bombs and taken ten photographs, came under attack from their old enemy *Jasta* 8 over Houthulst. Luchford and Kennard were credited with an Albatros in flames, as were Lt H W Joclyn and Pte F A Potter. In addition, 2Lt R M Makepeace and Lt M W Waddington got an Albatros OOC.

Jasta 8 became reluctant to press home its attacks after that, for the 'Fees' had brought down two of its aces. Ltn Alfred Ulmer, with five victories, crashed in flames, and although rescued from his demolished Albatros D V, died of his injuries soon after. Ltn Göttsch's D V spun down trailing smoke, and although he survived unhurt, he was understandably shaken up – this was not the first time that he had suffered at the hands of No 20 Sqn!

'ACEDOM' OVER HOME TURF

While FE 2bs and FE 2ds were fighting their last desperate dogfights over the Western Front, two British pusher types were scoring a spectacular success over their home ground. On the night of 16 June 1917, the Germans launched six of their newest class of high-altitude Zeppelins, called 'Height Climbers' by the British, on a bombing raid on London.

High cross-winds and engine trouble kept all but *L42* and *L48* from reaching England, and with a thunderstorm threatening to the west, *L42's* commander, Kapitänleutnant Martin Dietrich, judged it prudent to attack Dover instead. Even then, a south-southeast wind caused his bombs to fall on Ramsgate instead, although one 660-lb bomb struck a naval

83

Although deemed to be too vulnerable for daylight operations over the Western Front by late 1917, FE 2b and FE 2c bombers continued to take the fight to the enemy after dark. This particular aircraft was assigned to No 100 Sqn, which eventually replaced its 'Fees' with Handley Page O/400s in August 1918 (*Aaron Weaver*)

ammunition depot, killing three civilians and wounding 14 civilians and two servicemen. Although pursued by three aircraft from the RNAS station at Great Yarmouth, *L42* managed to return safely to base the next morning.

L48, serving as flagship for the raid (with deputy commander of airships Korvettenkapitän Victor Schutze aboard), was having more trouble. Suffering from both a frozen compass and unserviceable starboard engine by the time it made landfall south of Orfordness, its commander chose to bomb Harwich at this point. However, *L48's* 13 bombs fell harmlessly in a field at Kirton, five miles to the north. While the Zeppelin struggled home at an altitude of 17,000 ft, three Home Defence aircraft that had been struggling up to this altitude attacked the airship simultaneously at 0325 hrs on 17 June.

The defenders were 2Lt L P Watkins in BE 12 6610 of No 37 Sqn, based at Goldhanger, in Essex, and two aircraft from the RFC's Experimental Station at Ordfordness – DH 2 A5058, flown by Capt R H M S Saundby, and FE 2b B401, crewed by 2Lt Frank Douglas Holder and Sgt Sydney Ashby. Their combined gunfire set the front and rear gas cells of *L48* ablaze and it fell to earth near Theberton, in Suffolk. Of its 18-man crew, only Ltn zur See Otto Meith and Machinist's Mate Heinrich Ellerkamm survived, the latter saved by the Zeppelin's collapsing aluminium structure as it hit the ground.

Saundby, Holder and Watkins were awarded the MC and Ashby the MM for their role in *L48's* destruction – Saundby had also finally achieved 'acedom' with this success. Serving postwar in Iraq and Aden, he earned the DFC in Egypt, served as Deputy Commander-in-Chief,

This photograph of *L48* was taken as the Zeppelin cruised over Friedrichshafen in the spring of 1917, and shortly before its ill-fated bombing sortie on 16-17 June (*Imperial War Museum*)

The pathetic remains of *L48* at Theberton, in Suffolk, on 17 June. Two cordons of soldiers keep curious onlookers at a safe distance while the bodies of the crew are recovered (*Imperial War Museum*)

Bomber Command, and retired in 1946 as Air Vice-Marshal Sir Robert Saundby KCB, KBE, MC, DFC, AFC. He died on 25 September 1971.

EXUENT NOT QUIETLY

A month after eliminating von Richthofen's man in *Jasta* 28, No 20 Sqn claimed the 'Red Baron' himself. At about 1030 hrs on 6 July, the unit was attacked over Wervicq by *Jasta* 11, and it claimed a total of seven enemy aeroplanes, four of which were credited to Lt D C Cunnell, then a

This FE 2b of No 51 Sqn was flown as a single-seat nightfighter by a detachment that the unit had established at Tydd St Mary, in Lincolnshire, in August 1917. It has one Lewis gun on a fixed mounting and another that could be aimed upwards. Both guns had illuminated pillar sights (*Phil Jarrett*)

flight commander, and 2Lt Albert Edward Woodbridge, in FE 2d A6512, two others to Luchford and Tennant in A6516 and one to the team of Lt Cecil Richards and 2Lt Albert Henry Wear in A6498. Woodbridge later recalled;

'Cunnell handled the old FE for all she was worth, banking her from one side to the other, ducking dives from above and missing head-on collisions by bare margins of feet. The air was full of whizzing machines, and the noise from the full-out motors and the crackling machine guns was more than defeaning. Cunnell and I fired into four of the Albatroses from as close as 30 yards, and I saw my tracers go right into their bodies. Those four went down. Some of them were on fire – just balls of smoke and flames, which was a nasty sight to see. Two of them came at us head-on, and the first one was von Richthofen. There wasn't a thing on that machine that wasn't red, and how he could fly!

'I opened fire with the front Lewis and so did Cunnell with the side gun. Cunnell held the FE on her course and so did the pilot of the all-red scout. With our combined speeds, we approached each other at 250 mph. I kept a steady stream of lead pouring into the nose of that machine. Then the Albatros pointed its nose down suddenly and passed under us. Cunnell banked and turned. We saw the all-red aeroplane slip into a spin. It turned over and over, round and round, completely out of control. His engine was going full on, so I figured I had at least wounded him. As his head was the only part that wasn't protected by his motor, I thought that's where he was hit.'

Von Richthofen's recollection of the incident suggests that the 'all-red' Albatros that Woodbridge saw was someone else's. Firstly, his D V 4693/17 only had the nose, upper wings, wheel hubs and tail painted

Having scored three victories flying DH 2s with No 24 Sqn in 1916 and one in an FE 8 with No 41 Sqn in 1917, Capt R H M S Saundby was again flying a thoroughly obsolete DH 2 on Home Defence duties when he finally 'made ace' in stunning fashion by sharing in the destruction of Zeppelin *L48* in the early hours of 17 June 1917 (*Norman Franks*)

red. Secondly, the 'Baron' was still approaching at 300 metres, and recalled being astounded to see the observer in the lead FE stand up and open fire at him at such a distance when, 'Suddenly there was a blow to my head! I was hit! For a moment I was completely paralysed throughout my whole body. My hands dropped to the side, my legs dangled inside the fuselage. The worst part was that the blow to the head had affected my optic nerve and I was completely blinded.'

Instinctively switching off his engine to minimise the danger of fire, von Richthofen had descended to an altitude of 800 metres before his vision began to return, at which point he restarted his motor and, noting that two of his men – Ltns d R Alfred Niederhoff and Otto Brauneck – had followed him down, landed in a field of high grass outside Wervicq. With a ten-centimetre-wide section of bone laid bare and a severe concussion, the 'Baron' was rushed to Field Hospital 76 at Courtrai, and subsequently convalesced at St Nicholas Hospital until 25 July when – though not fully healed – he rejoined JG I at Marckebeke.

The medical examination suggested that the round that glanced off von Richthofen's skull may in fact have come from behind, from one of his own men reacting to Wainwright's long shot. The English gunner – who, given the amount of lead flying about from various angles, could just as likely have been Tennant or Wear as Wainwright – therefore possibly played a more indirect role in temporarily depriving the 'Flying Circus' of its 'ringmaster' than was originally thought.

Still another possible source of the bullet with the 'Baron's' name on it could have been one of four Sopwith Triplanes of 'B' Flight, No 10 Sqn RNAS, flown by Flt Lts Raymond Collishaw and William Melville

Credited with seven victories whilst assigned to No 20 Sqn, including four on 6 July 1917, 2Lt Albert Edward Woodbridge is most celebrated for being credited with wounding von Richthofen on 6 July 1917. However, the 'Red Baron' may in fact have been more of an indirect victim of Woodbridge's long shot, having possibly been struck in error by one of his own men (*Norman Franks*)

Alexander, and Flt Sub-Lts Ellis V Reid and Desmond F Fitzgibbon. After departing Droglandt at 0940 hrs British time, Collishaw reported spotting 'and encounter between FEs and a number of enemy scouts', which Reid counted as 15.

Collishaw reported that he and his men 'dived and went into the fight', and in the ensuing 'general engagement' claimed nine Albatros, of which four were credited as 'out of control'. Aside from the optimistic claiming (Collishaw claimed an Albatros D V destroyed at 1100 hrs and five OOC at 1110, which

After suffering a head wound during an encounter with FE 2ds of No 20 Sqn on 6 July 1917, Rittm Manfred von Richthofen makes a reassuring public emergence from St Nicholas' Hospital, with Nurse Kätie Otersdorf in vigilant attendance. (*Imperial War Museum*)

his unit recorded as one OOC and five 'apparently out of control'), the time at which he alleged to have achieved his successes is not in synch with 1030 hrs, when Cunnell and Wainwright claimed their four.

In any case, with the very notable exception of von Richthofen, JG I recorded no casualties to remotely match the seven Albatros D Vs credited to No 20 Sqn and the four awarded to 'Naval 10' that day. Even allowing for the perception of Niederhoff and Brauneck descending to observe the forced landing of their *Geschwaderkommandeur* as two more OOCs, that leaves a lot of benefit of the doubt to be allowed. Under the circumstances, Cunnell and Woodbridge are neither more nor less valid candidates than anyone else involved for the credit officially given them for temporarily putting the 'Red Baron' out of action,

Promoted to captain after the action, Cunnell – with Lt A G Bill as his observer – was credited with an Albatros in flames between Wervicq and Menin on 11 July for his ninth victory. During another combat over Wervicq the next day, he was killed by anti-aircraft fire, but Lt Bill managed to take control of A6412 and fly it back to base. Cunnell was buried at the Bailleul Communal Cemetery Extension.

Woodbridge survived to sit in the back seat of a Bristol Fighter, claiming three more victories in concert with 2Lt William Durrand. After the war he became a pilot, and following several years in civil aviation, rejoined the RAF but fatally crashed during a night landing attempt at Jask, in Persia, on 7 September 1929.

July saw Richards and Wear adding to their scores – 12 for the former and nine for the latter by mid-August. Luchford also brought his total up to 11 during that time, four of which were claimed with Lt M W Waddington and two with Tennant.

In August 1917 Bristol F 2Bs began arriving at No 20 Sqn. Given the aggressiveness with which so many of its veterans had handled their 'Fees', their transition to the faster and more agile Bristol was remarkably smooth. The same could be said for the squadron mechanics, already experienced with the Roll-Royce engines that the FE 2d and the F 2B had in common. Even so, a flying accident in newly delivered F 2B A7108 killed Capt Arthur Solly and Lt D Y Hay on 11 August. Yorkshire-born Solly had scored his first two victories as an FE 2b observer with No 23 Sqn in 1916, and another seven as an FE 2d pilot in 20 Sqn – the last two the day before he died, aged 23.

The first No 20 Sqn men to score in the Bristol, downing an Albatros D V on 3 September, were Lts R M Makepeace and M W Waddington. Born in Liverpool on 27 December 1887, Reginald Milburn Makepeace was a Canadian resident when war broke out. Posted to 20 Sqn on 8 June 1917, he scored his first eight victories in FE 2ds while the 21-year-old, Toronto-born Melville Wells Waddington, a former member of the Canadian Field Artillery, had seven. In F 2Bs Makepeace and Waddington added three more to their scores together, and Makepeace would ultimately raise his total to 17, only to die in a flying accident at Turnberry aerodrome on 28 May 1918. William Durrand, credited with four enemy aeroplanes destroyed piloting FE 2ds, doubled that number after switching to the Bristol – three came in concert with Albert Woodbridge.

On 9 September Lt Luchford, with Lt Richard Frank Hill in the observer's pit, drove an Albatros down OOC near Becelaere. It was the first of 13 victories he would score in the Bristol before being shot down and killed by Ltn Walter von Bülow of *Jasta* 36 on 4 December 1917, his observer, Capt J E Johnston, surviving as a PoW.

By the time it exchanged the last of its pushers for Bristols, No 20 Sqn had been credited with 203 victories over enemy aircraft. It would raise that total to 619 in the tractor two-seaters – a wartime record, although only a fraction of its claims, in FE and Bristol alike, can be matched by postwar documentation of enemy losses.

The versatile FE 2bs and FE 2ds saw another year of service over the Western Front as night bombers, often making life miserable anew for the *Jagdflieger* at their aerodromes. Even after their withdrawal from this theatre, a few DH 2s turned up for a time in Palestine and Macedonia. By the end of 1917, however, the pusher fighter and the exceptional airmen who rode them into battle was a closed chapter in the history of aerial warfare – at least until 1944, when a new type of 'pusher' fighter, propelled by jet power, burst upon the scene to open a new era.

Hailing from Bromley, in Kent, Lt H G E Luchford was among No 20 Sqn's leading lights, being credited with 11 victories in FE 2ds in the summer of 1917 and 13 thereafter in Bristol F 2Bs. On 4 December 1917, however, he was shot down and killed by Ltn Walter von Bülow of *Jasta* 36, his observer, Capt J E Johnston, surviving as a PoW (*Norman Franks*)

APPENDICES

FB 5, FE 2b and FE 2d Aces

Pilot	Squadron(s)	Score in Types	Total	Aircraft serial(s)
J V Aspinall	22 & 11	5	6	FE 2b A4983
C M Clement	22	8	14	FE 2b A5461
R E Conder	20	6	6	FE 2d A6415
D C Cunnell	20	9	9	FE 2d A6512
H B Davey	25 & 11	6	6	FE 2b A5238
C S Duffus	22 & 25	5	5	FE 2b A6931
J H Green	25	5	5	FE 2b A6990
H E Hartney	22	6	7	FE 2b A1960
V H Huston	18	6	6	FE 2bs A4865 & A4998
H W Joclyn	20	7	7	FE 2d A6415
J L Leith	25 & 46	8	9	FE 2bs A7693 & A782
H G E Luchford	20	11	24	FE 2ds A6516 & A6548
R M Makepeace	20 & 11	8	17	FE 2d A6458
R G Malcolm	25	8	8	FE 2b A7672
S W Price	23, 11, 33 & 36	7	7	FE 2b A6994
J B Quested	11 & 40	8	8	FE 2b A6965
L W B Rees	11 & 32	6	8	FB 5 A1649 & DH 2 A6015
G R M Reid	25, 20, 18 & 206	9	9	FE 2b A6330 & FE 2d A39
G P S Reid	20	5	5	FE 2d A19
C R Richards	20	12	12	FE 2ds A6498 & A6468
L L Richardson	25	7	7	FE 2b A4283
H L Satchell	20	8	8	FE 2ds A6469 & A6431
A N Solly	23 & 20	9	9	FE 2ds A6354 & A5147
F D Stevens	20	5	5	FE 2d A6516
D A Stewart	20 & 18	16	16	FE 2b A8038
F J H Thayer	16 & 20	19	20	FE 2d A6430
R M Trevethan	20	12	12	FE 2d A6528
O H D Vickers	20	13	13	FE 2d A6376
C H C Woollven	25	5	5	FE 2b A7024

Observer	Squadron(s)	Score in Types	Total	Aircraft serial(s)
G N Blennerhasset	18	6	6	FE 2b A7003
W C Cambray	20	5	6	FE 2d A6516
L S Court	25	8	8	FE 2b A6932
J J Cowell	20	15	16	FE 2ds A6415 & A6376
F R Cubbon	20	21	21	FE 2d A6430
L H Emsden	25	8	8	FE 2b A7672
W T Gilson	20	5	5	FE 2d A29
J M Hargreaves	11	5	5	FB 5 A1649
J A Hoy	20	6	6	FE 2d A6528
C A Hoy	20	10	10	FE 2d A6528
F J Kydd	20	5	5	FE 2d A5147
A N Jenks	20	7	7	FE 2d A6431
T A M S Lewis	20	6	6	FE 2d A6412
F Libby	23, 11, 43 & 25	10	14	FE 2b A6994
M K Parlee	22	6	6	FE 2d A5461
L H Scott	20	6	6	FE 2ds A22 & A39
J R Smith	18	5	5	FE 2b A5464
J Tennant	20	7	7	FE 2d A6512
M W Waddington	20	7	12	FE 2d A6548
A E Wear	20	9	9	FE 2ds A6498 & B1890
A E Woodbridge	20	4	7	FE 2d A6512

DH 2 and FE 8 Aces

Pilot	Squadron(s)	Score in Types	Total	Aircraft serial(s)
J O Andrews	24, 66 & 209	7	12	DH 2 A5998
E L Benbow	40 & 85	8	8	FE 8s A7627 & A4871
S Cockerell	24	5	6	DH 2 A2581
S E Cowan	24 & 29	7	7	DH 2 A5964
W G S Curphey	32	6	6	DH 2 A2536
H C Evans	24	5	5	DH 2 A7878
H W G Jones	32	7	7	DH 2s A2553 & A7882
A G Knight	4, 24 & 29	8	8	DH 2 A5931
P A Langan-Byrne	24	10	10	DH 2 A7911
S H Long	29, 24, 46 & 111	9	9	DH 2 A305
J T B McCudden	3, 20, 29, 66 & 56	5	57	DH 2 A7858
E C Pashley	24	8	8	DH 2 A7930
R H M S Saundby	24, 41 & HD	5	5	DH 2 A5058
A M Wilkinson	24, 48 & 23	10	19	DH 2 A5966
H A Wood	24, 48 & 23	5	5	DH 2 A7918

Artist Harry Dempsey has created the colour profiles for this volume, working closely with the author to portray the aircraft despicted as accurately as circumstances permit. Some of the illustrations are, admittedly, reconstructions based on fragmentary photographic evidence or descriptions provided by the pilots while they were alive, combined with known unit marking policy.

1

Voisin 3LA V89 of Sgt Joseph Frantz and Soldat Louis Quénault, V24, Lery, October 1914

Powered by a 130 hp Salmson Canton-Unné engine and one of six in the escadrille to be fitted with Hotchkiss machine guns, Voisin V89 made history on 5 October 1914 when Frantz and his observer Quénault shot down Albatros B II B114/14 near Reims, killing Sgt Wilhelm Schilling and Oblt Fritz von Zangen of Flieger Abteilung 18.

2

Voisin 3LAS V647 of Adj Charles Nungesser and Soldat Roger Pochon, VB106, Dunkerque, July 1915

Adj Nungesser collected V361 at Le Bourget on 6 June 1915 and flew it through to 1 August. This was probably the machine he decorated with the first version of his soon-to-be familiar death's head emblem, but he and his mechanic – and frequent observer – Pochon may have 'borrowed' another aeroplane on the night of 31 July, when they shot down one of five Albatros two-seaters staging a nocturnal raid on Nancy. For making an unauthorised flight, Nungesser was confined to quarters for eight days. For scoring his first victory, he was awarded the Croix de Guerre, and transferred to fighters, in which he would add 42 more to his tally.

3

Maurice Farman MF 11bis (serial unknown) of Lts Fernand Jacquet and Louis Robin, 1ère Escadrille, St-Idesbald, May 1916

With its visored prow decorated with a variation on Jacquet's death's head, this Farman was flown by him and Robin when they intercepted ten German naval aircraft en route to bomb De Panne on 20 May 1916, and sent one of their adversaries crashing into the sea off Nieuport.

4

Georges Nélis GN 2 (serial unknown) of Capt Fernand Jacquet and Lt Louis Robin, 1ère Escadrille, Les Moëres, February 1917

Jacquet became Belgium's first ace in this aeroplane on 1 February 1917, when he and Robin shot down a brown Rumpler that crashed at Lomardszijde. Their victim may have been from FFA, which reported observer Ltn Fritz Patheiger killed near Polygon Forest. Jacquet scored two more victories in SPAD XIs in 1918.

5

Vickers FB 5 1649 of Capt Lionel W B Rees and Flt Sgt J M Hargreaves, No 11 Sqn, Vert Galand, July 1915

Joining the RFC on 10 August 1914, the aggressive Lionel Rees flew this Bristol-built FB 5 with No 11 Sqn in the summer of 1915. On 28 July he and his observer, Flt Sgt J M Hargreaves, drove down a Fokker E I, followed by two-seaters on 31 August and 21, 22 and 30 September, for which Rees was awarded the MC and Hargreaves the DCM. On 31 October Rees and Flt Sgt Raymond downed an LVG, making the former the only pilot to achieve 'acedom' flying the Vickers Gunbus.

6

Vickers FB 5 5074 of Lt Gilbert Stuart Martin Insall and AM T H Donald, No 11 Sqn, Villers Bretonneux, November 1915

On 7 November Insall was flying Darracq-built FB 5 5074, with AM T H Donald as his observer, when they forced an Aviatik to land southeast of Arras. Ignoring ground fire – including shots from the German crew, at whom Donald returned fire – Insall dropped a small incendiary bomb that set the Aviatik afire. On the way home they strafed the German trenches, but their petrol tank was hit. Insall landed in a wood 500 yards inside Allied lines, where he and Donald stood by their aeroplane despite enemy shellfire. They spent the night repairing the petrol tank and duly 5074 back to their aerodrome the next morning. Insall was awarded the VC and Donald the DCM for this action.

7

FE 2b 6994 of Capt Stephen W Price and Lt Frederick Libby, No 11 Sqn, Isel-le-Hameau, September 1916

Built by Boulton & Paul Ltd, FE 2b 6994 bore the presentation legend MONTREAL No 3 on the nacelle. Price, who commanded 'B' Flight, scored five of his seven victories in this aeroplane, with Libby as his observer – three Roland C IIs on 22 August 1916, an Aviatik on the 25th and a two-seater on 14 September, for which both crewmen were awarded the MC. Three days later, 'C' Flight crew 2Lt H Thompson and Sgt J E Glover 'borrowed' 6994 and were shot down and killed near Equancourt by ace Ltn Wilhelm Frankl of Jasta 4. After being credited with ten victories (making him the first American ace of the war, albeit not a pilot), Fred Libby took flight training and subsequently scored two victories flying Sopwith 1½ Strutters with No 43 Sqn and two in DH 4s with No 25 Sqn in 1917.

8

FE 2b 4969 of 2Lts V H Huston and G N Blennerhasset, No 18 Sqn, Isel-le-Hameau, April 1917

No 18 Sqn proposed adorning the nacelles of its FE 2bs with a red triangle, but the RFC disapproved of the marking, declaring it unnecessary. Photographs nevertheless reveal a lozenge-shaped device in a shade too light to be red (which looks very dark on orthochromatic film), but which may be yellow, with wheel hubs seemingly in the same colour. The reconstructed scheme shown here is admittedly hypothetical. In addition to that marking, FE 2b 4969 bore the presentation legend SHANGHAI No 3 SHANGHAI EXHIBITION. 2Lts V H Huston and G N Blennerhasset used it to drive two Albatros D IIs down OOC over Inchy – the second and third victories for both men. 4969 crashed on 16 April, but was repaired and served with No 102 Sqn until 9 October 1917, when Lt D Powell and RF Hill went missing in it. Born in Ireland on 18 October 1890, Victor Henry Huston was living in Vancouver, Canada when war broke out, and he served with No 18 Sqn from 17 December 1916 through to 8 July 1917. He scored his fifth and sixth victories in 4998 CEYLON No 3 A NIGHTJAR FROM CEYLON on 13 and 27 May to become the unit's only FE 2b ace pilot, and was awarded the MC. After attaining the rank of major, and chief instructor, in the new Chilean Air Force, Huston left the RAF in November 1919. Joining No 18 Sqn after previously serving in the 4th Royal Irish Rifles, 2Lt Giles Noble Blennerhasset scored his first victory with 2Lt Robert W Farquhar (later to claim five more victories in SPAD VIIs) on 4 February 1917. On 23 May Blennerhasset, as observer to 2Lt D E Marshall in FE 2b 7003, downed two Albatros D IIIs to take his final tally to eight.

9

FE 2b 4883 of Capt Chester Stairs Duffus and 2Lt G O McEntee, No 22 Sqn, Bertangles, December 1916

While flying the G & J Weir-built FE 2b 4883 KOOKABURRA, Duffus and McEntee were credited with an Albatros D I down out of control over Barastre on 4 December 1916. Their victim was possibly Offstv Karl Ernthaller of Jasta 1, whose body was found in Fokker D I 175/16 near Provin. 4883 was subsequently forced to land near Bapaume, but was restored to flight status. Flying 7697 on 11 December, Duffus and McEntee and another FE 2b crew shared in a two-seater in flames again near Bapaume, bringing Duffus' score up to five. He subsequently commanded No 25 Sqn, and survived the war with the rank of major. FE 2b 4883's career ended on 26 April 1917, when Offstv Alfred Sturm of Jasta 5 brought it down, Capt H Rupert Hawkins and 2Lt McEntee being made PoWs.

10

FE 2b A5461 of Capt Carleton Main Clement and 2Lt Medley Kingdon Parlee, No 22 Sqn, Trecon, May 1917

This Boulton & Paul-built aeroplane bore the presentation MONTREAL No 2 on its nacelle and probably 'C' Flight leader's markings as shown. Its regular pilot, Capt Carleton M Clement, scored eight victories in FE 2bs, including an Albatros D III destroyed near Rocquigny in A5461 on 4 February 1917. Clement and 2Lt Llewelyn Crichton Davies shared in the destruction of a D III with other FEs on 6 April, probably killing Vzfw Reinhold Wurzmann of Jasta 20, and downed another DIII two days later. Still in A5461, Clement and fellow Canadian M K Parlee destroyed two D IIIs on 9 May (taking Parlee's final tally to six). On 5 June Clement and Davies claimed an Albatros destroyed and one OOC northwest of Lesdains, bringing the observer's total to five – and mortally wounding Ltn Kurt Schneider, 15-victory ace and acting commander of Jasta 5. A5461 was transferred to No 101 Sqn in July 1917, but was written off after a crash on 10 September. After No 22 Sqn replaced its FEs with Bristol F 2B fighters, Clement raised his total to 14, but on 19 August he and his observer, Lt R B Carter, were killed by anti-aircraft fire near Langemarck.

11

FE 2b 6993 of Lt Noel W W Webb and Sgt Leslie S Court, No 25 Sqn, St Achelle, September 1916

This Boulton & Paul-built machine, inscribed with the presentation BARODA No 14 on its nacelle, was used by 2Lt Alwyne Travers Loyd (a 21-year-old Kentish-born, Eton-educated Welshman) and 2Lt C S Workman to drive a Fokker Eindecker OOC on 7 September 1916. Loyd scored a second victory with No 22 Sqn on 4 December, and four more in DH 5s with No 32 Sqn, before he was killed east of Ypres on 28 September 1917, either by flak or by Oblt Rudolf Berthold of Jasta 18. On 9 September Lt N W W Webb and Sgt Leslie S Court were flying in 6993 when they destroyed a two-seater near Pont a Vendin. This was the fourth victory for the 19-year-old Webb, from Kensington, in London, since he joined No 25 Sqn on 4 July 1916. After scoring a fifth over a Fokker E III near Fresnoy on 15 September in concert with Workman, Webb was awarded the MC. Following time back in England, he returned to the front with Sopwith Camel-equipped No 70 Sqn, raising his total to 14 before being killed by Ltn Werner Voss of Jasta 10 on 16 August 1917. The victory on 9 September 1916 was Leslie Court's fifth of an eventual eight, which earned him a French Médaille Militaire. On 22 September, however, FE 2b 6993 was brought down near Combles by Ltn Hans-Joachim Buddecke of Jasta 4, 2Lt K F Hunt and Cpl L O Law being taken prisoner.

12

FE 2d A'39 of Capt George R M Reid and Lt Laurence H Scott, No 20 Sqn, Clairmarais, October 1916

Born in Scotland on 25 October 1893, George Ranald Macfarlane Reid had served in the Argyll and Sutherland Highlanders and the Black Watch, prior to transferring to the RFC in August 1915. Serving in No 25 Sqn from February 1916, he and Lt James Anderson Mann scored three victories in FE 2b 6330, earning them the MC, before Reid transferred to No 20 Sqn as a captain and flight commander. With 20-year-old Lt Laurence Henry Scott, from Balham, South London, as his usual observer, Reid scored six more victories, the last three of which, on 16 September and 16 and 21 October, were in Royal Aircraft Factory built FE 2d A'39. Awarded a bar to his MC, Reid alternated between training assignments in England and command of bomber units' Nos 18 and 206 Sqns, receiving the DSO for his work on 1 January 1919. He retired from the RAF in 1946 as Air Vice-Marshal Sir Ranald Reid KCB, and moved to Western Australia. Meanwhile, A'39 had been assigned to Lt Harold E Hartney – his eighth 'Fee' since he had joined the squadron – but on 7 January 1917 he 'loaned' it to Flt Sgt Mottershead. During the day's mission it was set afire by Vfw Walter Göttsch of Jasta 8, the subsequent actions of its crew to land their burning machine earning an MC for the observer, Lt W E Gower, and a posthumous VC for Mottershead.

13

FE 2d A6430 of Capts Frederick James Harry Thayre and Francis Richard Cubbon, No 20 Sqn, Lemmes, May 1917

The first of a series of aircraft inscribed with the name of AJMEER (the Indian province that helped finance its construction), Boulton & Paul-built A6430 and its crew, Capt F J H Thayre and Francis R Cubbon, formed a conquering triumvirate that was credited with no fewer than 20 victories between 29 April and 7 June 1917. This remarkable run of luck abruptly ran out two days later when A6430 was destroyed by a direct shell hit from K Flak 60.

14

FE 2d A6516 of Capt Frank Douglas Stevens and Lt William C Cambray, No 20 Sqn, Clairmarais, July 1917

Bearing the legend Presented by the COLONY OF MAURITIUS NO 13, this Boulton & Paul-built machine was used by Lt H G E Luchford and 2Lt James Tennant to drive down an Albatros D III OOC near Houthem on 13 June 1917, and by Luchford and 2Lt W D Kennard to destroy a D III in flames near Zonnebeke on the 29th. The FE was piloted by 'Inky' Stevens when he and Lt Frederick J Kydd downed an Albatros D III on 3 July (his second and Kydd's fifth, and last, victory), and when he and Lt A N Jenks claimed another on 6 July. Stevens and Cambray teamed up to down D IIIs in A6516 on 17 July and 16 August, bringing the former's total to five, but combat damage on 20 September led to the aeroplane being struck off charge six days later.

15

FE 2d A6528 of 2Lt Richard Michael Trevethan and Lt Campbell Alexander Hoy, No 20 Sqn, Lemmes, July 1917

Another Boulton & Paul FE 2d, A6528 was given the presentation legend AUSTRALIA NO 12 – NSW NO 11 – THE MACINTIRE KAYUGA ESTATE on 4 June 1917 and assigned to No 20 Sqn until struck off in August. Its first success (an Albatros D V on 7 July) was the fourth for 2Lt R M Trevethan and the third for Lt C M Hoy. The latter, who had served in the Northern Cyclist Battalion, Territorial Force, before joining the RFC, had been injured on 25 May 1917 when FE 2d A6366 was shot down in Allied lines by Ltn August Hanko of Jasta 28, his pilot, 2Lt Baring-Gould, also being wounded. Hoy first got revenge while flying with Lt J R Patteron in A6547 (AUSTRALIA NO 13 – NSW NO 11 – THE MACINTIRE KAYUGA ESTATE) when they destroyed an Albatros D V over Becelaère on 29 June. Richard M Trevethan, who had been born in the United States on 24 January 1895, but whose nationality was British, teamed up with Hoy in A6512 to down a D V on 17 July, in A6528 again to score on the 22nd and 28th, and in A6527 for two D V victories on 8 August. A final success the next day took Trevethan's tally to 12, and Hoy's to 10. Trevethan later served in North Russia in 1919, and was a squadron leader at RAF Henlow in 1934.

16

DH 2 5966 of Capt Alan M Wilkinson, No 24 Sqn, Bertangles, August 1916

Born in Eastbourne, Sussex, on 21 November 1891, Oxford educated and previously serving with the Hampshire Regiment of the Territorial Force, Alan Machin Wilkinson was one of No 24 Sqn's first aces. He scored six victories in DH 2 5966, including doubles on 16 May and 17 June 1916, before being slightly wounded on 20 June. Although it is uncertain which of his aeroplanes was photographed bearing the unusual segmented wheel hub variation of 'C' Flight's marking, they are depicted here on 5966, in which Wilkinson scored the first six of his ten DH 2 victories between 16 May and 19 July 1916. Later flying Bristol F 2As with No 48 Sqn, Wilkinson brought his total to 19 in April 1917.

17

DH 2 5964 of Maj Lanoe G Hawker, No 24 Sqn, Bertangles, November 1916

Sidney Edward Cowan was flying 5964 on 1 July 1916 when he downed a two-seater OOC and on 16 September when he was credited with a Fokker in flames. Maj Hawker was at the controls on 23 November when he had his fateful encounter with Ltn Manfred von Richthofen of Jasta 2.

18

DH 2 A305 of Capt Seldon Herbert Long, No 24 Sqn, Bertangles, March 1917

After serving in the Durham Light Infantry, 'Tubby' Long joined the RFC and scored his first victory with No 29 Sqn on 9 August 1916. Transferring to No 24 Sqn, he had claimed a further seven victories by the end of January 1917, five in A305. His aeroplane is reconstructed as it probably looked after he became 'C' Flight leader, with the individual aircraft numbers being adopted in early 1917. On 6 March Long, in A305, shared his last victory with 2Lt E C Pashley, before returning to Home Establishment. Meanwhile, Capt Hubert W G Jones of No 32 Sqn had transferred to No 24 Sqn on 11 March to take command of 'C' Flight, and A305, but he had failed to add to his tally of seven victories by the time he was brought down wounded in British lines near Roupy by Ltns W Olsen and W Hilf of Fl Abt 32 on the evening of 21 March.

19

DH 2 7858 of Flt Sgt J T B McCudden, No 29 Sqn, Abeele, September 1916

Born in Gillingham, Kent, on 28 March 1895, James Thomas Byford McCudden joined the Royal Engineers in 1910, transferred to the RFC as a mechanic in 1913 and served as an observer in No 3 Sqn, before becoming a pilot on FE 2ds with No 20 Sqn in July 1916. Switching to DH 2s in No 29 Sqn a month later, he was flying 7858 with the blue wheel hub of 'C' Flight when he scored his first victory over a two-seater on 6 September. Later that month McCudden's aeroplane was further marked with a blue number (unfortunately unknown) on the nacelle and wings . On 27 December McCudden was driven down to 800 ft by a persistent Albatros, but managed to return to base unhurt, much to the amazement of his squadron mates who had given him up for lost – as did the Germans, who apparently credited him as the 15th victory for Ltn Manfred von Richthofen of Jasta 2. McCudden resumed scoring in DH 2 7858 on 26 January 1917, bringing his total to five on 15 February and earning him an MC. Later serving in Nos 66 and 56 Sqns, McCudden had taken his tally to 57 by 26 February 1918, subsequently receiving the VC and command of No 60 Sqn. He was fatally injured in a flying accident on 10 July 1918.

20

DH 2 6015 of Maj Lionel W B Rees, No 32 Sqn, Treizennes, July 1916

Shown with 'A' flight wheel hubs, since that flight shared quarters with No 32 Sqn's HQ personnel at Treizennes, DH 2 6015 was flown by No 32 Sqn's CO on 1 July 1916 when he took on up to ten Roland C IIs, and was credited with two of them destroyed before being wounded in the leg. Rees was awarded the VC for his bravery. Sgt Eric H Dobson was reportedly shot down in flames in 6015 near Faucourt l'Abbé on 12 August, Gwilym H Lewis recalling in his diary, 'The other day Sgt Dobson separated himself from his patrol and was seen to be shot down by four Rolands who slunk up behind him'.

21

DH 2 A2553 of Capt Hubert Wilson Godfrey Jones, No 32 Sqn, Treizennes, September 1916

Earning the MC with the Welsh Regiment prior to joining the RFC and No 32 Sqn, Hubert Jones opened his account with a Fokker Eindecker OOC on 11 August 1916 whilst flying A2553 – shown here with 'B' Flight wheel hubs. He also used it to destroy an LVG on 23 September and down another two-seater OOC on 1 October. Flying 7882 on 16 November, Jones shared in the downing of two more two-seaters OOC with Lt M J J G Mare-Montembault, and finished his scoring with Albatros D Is on 5 and 15 February 1917. On 21 March he was wounded when shot down in Allied lines in DH 2 A305 by Ltns W Olsen and W Hilf of *Fl Abt* 23. Upon recovery, Jones served at the Central Flying School, then twice as commander of No 19 Sqn (from November 1918 to December 1919 and from 1925 to 1928), before retiring from the RAF as a major.

22

FE 8 7457 of Capt Frederick J Powell, No 5 Sqn, Abeele, January 1916

Sent to No 5 Sqn for evaluation on 26 December 1915, the second prototype FE 8 was flown exclusively by Capt Frederick James Powell MC, who had two previous victories on FB 5s. Flying 7457 on 17 January 1916, Powell sent an Aviatik down OOC near Becelaere. Of the three claims he made on 5 February, an LVG 'driven down' was credited to him, as was an Aviatik in flames on 29 February and a Fokker Eindecker 'driven down' on 12 March.

23

FE 8 6388 of 2Lt John Hay, No 40 Sqn, Treizennes, January 1917

Although Lt Edwin Benbow was the only pilot to become an ace in the FE 8, fellow No 40 Sqn pilot Australian 2Lt 'Jack' Hay claimed three victories in the fighter. His last, an Albatros two-seater, was downed at 1015 hrs on 23 January 1917. During an escort patrol latter that same day, his Darracq-built FE 8 (6388) was seen falling in flames at 1505 hrs. Hay's remains were recovered by Canadian troops two miles east of Aix Noulette. He had become the 17th victim of Ltn Manfred von Richthofen, and the first for the 'Red Baron's' new command, *Jasta* 11.

24

FE 8 7626 of Lt K M St C G Leask, No 41 Sqn, Abeele, January 1917

Shown after 26 January 1917, when Leask was promoted to the temporary rank of captain and made commander of 'B' Flight, FE 8 7626, built by Vickers Ltd, shows typical numeral placement adopted by No 41 Sqn. Born on 30 October 1896 in Southsea, Hampshire, Kenneth Malice St Clair Graeme Leask entered the RFC in May 1916, flying BEs with No 42 Sqn until his transfer to No 41 Sqn in December. He scored no confirmed victories in the FE 8 prior to departing the unit to become a flight instructor in May 1917. Leask was later made commander of No 84 Sqn's 'A' Flight when it received SE 5as in August 1917, and was credited with eight victories flying the fighter between 21 October 1917 and 23 March 1918. Retiring as an air vice marshal, Leask was tragically killed, along with his wife, in an automobile accident on 24 April 1974.

BIBLIOGRAPHY

Bowyer, Chaz, *For Valour - The Air VCs*, Grub Street, London, 1992

Bruce, J M, *The Airco DH 2*, Profile Publications, Ltd, Leatherhead, Surrey, 1966

Bruce, J M, *RAF FE 8*, Albatros Productions Ltd, Berkhamsted, Herts, 1999

Bruce, J M, *Vickers FB 5*, Albatros Productions Ltd, Berkhamsted, Herts, 1996

Chidlaw-Roberts, Robert Leslie and Tappin, David, 'Chidlaw, Just an Ordinary Humdrum Pilot', *Cross & Cockade International Journal*, Vol 20, No 2, pp 57-67, Autumn 1987

Coppens, Baron Willy, 'Belgian Aviation 1914-1918', *Cross & Cockade Journal* (USA), Vol 5, No 2, pp 105-108, Spring 1964

Franks, Norman, *Sharks Among the Minnows*, Grub Street, London, 2001

Franks, Norman, Bailey, Frank and Duiven, Rick, *The Jasta War Chronology*, Grub Street, London, 1998

Franks, Norman, Guest, Russell and Bailey, Frank, *Bloody April . . . Black September*, Grub Street, London, 1995

Franks, Norman, Gilpin, Hal and McCrery, Nigel, *Under the Guns of the Red Baron*, Grub Street, London, 1995

Hartney, Harold E, *Up & At 'Em*, Ace Books, New York, NY, 1971

Holder, Sqn Ldr F D, 'The Destruction of the *L48*,' *Cross & Cockade (Great Britain) Journal*, Vol 7, No 3, pp 103-110, Autumn 1976

Kilduff, Peter, *Richthofen - Beyond the Legend of the Red Baron*, Arms & Armour Press, London, 1993

Lewis, Wg Cdr Gwilym H, *Wings over the Somme, 1916-1918*, William Kimber & Co, Ltd, London, 1976

Libby, Frederick, *Horses Don't Fly - A Memoir of World War I*, Arcade Publishing, New York, NY, 2000

McCudden, Maj James T B, *Flying Fury - Five Years in the Royal Flying Corps*, Ace Publishing, New York, NY, 1968

Miller, James F, 'Eagles vs Butterflies - Manfred on Ricthofen's Wounding, 6 July 1917', *Over the Front*, Vol 23, No 3, pp 196-214, Autumn 2008

Miller, James F, 'Eight Minutes Near Bapaume', *Over the Front*, Vol 21, No 2, pp 120-138, Summer 2006,

Revell, Alex, *British Single-Seater Fighter Squadrons on the Western Front in World War I*, Schiffer Publishing Ltd, Atglen, Pa, 2006

Shores, Christopher, Franks, Norman, and Guest, Russell, *Above the Trenches*, Grub Street, London, 1990

INDEX

References to illustrations are shown in **bold**. Plates are shown with page and caption locators in brackets.